"I especially appreciate how Lohfink reveals the Jewishness of the prayer. I'll continue to say these words in traditional form at Mass, and in times of personal prayer, but I understand them better than ever before."

> —Jon M. Sweeney
> Editor of *A Course in Christian Mysticism* by Thomas Merton

"The Our Father is our prayer taught by our Lord himself. Gerhard Lohfink has brought forward the most comprehensive interpretation from his vast and timely biblical scholarship. I found this book to be an awakening.

"The Our Father is a deeper prayer than I have known. Lofink teaches a practice of eschatology. This reign of God at-work-now is most urgent in our times. This book is ideal for preachers and teachers in our Church."

> —Mary Margaret Funk, OSB
> Author of *Renouncing Violence: Practice from the Monastic Tradition*

# THE OUR FATHER

## *A New Reading*

Gerhard Lohfink

Translated by Linda M. Maloney

**LITURGICAL PRESS**
Collegeville, Minnesota

www.litpress.org

Excerpt from the English translation of *The Roman Missal, Third Edition* © 2010, International Commission on English in the Liturgy Corporation (ICEL). All rights reserved.

© 2012, 2019 Verlag Katholisches Bibelwerk GmbH, Stuttgart. Translated from the 3rd ed., 2015.

| 1 | 2 | 3 | 4 | 5 | 6 | 7 | 8 | 9 |
|---|---|---|---|---|---|---|---|---|

**Library of Congress Cataloging-in-Publication Data**

Names: Lohfink, Gerhard, 1934– author.
Title: The Our Father : a new reading / Gerhard Lohfink ;
    translated by Linda M. Maloney.
Other titles: Vaterunser neu ausgelegt. English
Description: Collegeville, Minnesota : Liturgical Press, 2019. |
    Includes bibliographical references.
Identifiers: LCCN 2018030690 (print) | LCCN 2018050959
    (ebook) | ISBN 9780814663844 (ebook) | ISBN
    9780814663592
Subjects: LCSH: Lord's prayer.
Classification: LCC BV230 (ebook) | LCC BV230 .L5413 2019
    (print) | DDC 226.9/606—dc23
LC record available at https://lccn.loc.gov/2018030690

To my brother Norbert

in gratitude

# CONTENTS

# PREFACE TO
# THE AMERICAN EDITION

Discussion of the correct translation and meaning of the sixth petition in the Our Father ("lead us not into temptation") is unending, and it has taken on a new life in our time. It shows how important the Our Father is to many Christians. They want to understand it. They want to know what they are really praying for.

This book is intended to serve that need. I ask about the original meaning of the Lord's Prayer because it is only when we are clear about what it meant in that time that we can apply it in our current situations.

I dedicate this little book to my brother Norbert: for good reasons! We have often talked about the right interpretation of the Our Father. On two occasions we have joined together to address conferences on our reading of it. In preparing for those conferences

I learned a great deal from my brother about the Old Testament background of the prayer, and that whole process has contributed to this book. It is a tiny token of gratitude for many mutual discussions.

I owe thanks also to my former student, Dr. Linda Maloney, who has applied her thorough knowledge of the state of the exegetical problem to the translation of the book. I hope it will help many people to enjoy praying the Our Father and to increase in their love for Jesus.

Gerhard Lohfink

# 1. The Curious Form of the Our Father

THE OUR FATHER is probably the prayer most often prayed throughout the world. But it is anything but a universal prayer. It is first of all and primarily a prayer for Jesus' disciples. Matthew places it at the center of the Sermon on the Mount—which is, as its introduction shows, addressed not only to the people in general but first and primarily to Jesus' disciples (cp. Matt 5:1-2). Luke makes it quite clear who the addressees are: in his gospel one of Jesus' disciples asks him:

> "Lord, teach us to pray, as John taught his disciples." (Luke 11:1)

But it is not only because of this information in Matthew and Luke that we know the Our Father as primarily a prayer for disciples. Its content shows that as well. This is clearest in the fourth petition, for bread, which seems to reflect the bitter situation of day laborers in Palestine and with it the misery of all the hungry and needy of this world. In reality the request for bread comes from the specific situation of Jesus' disciples, which had to do with their duty to preach and proclaim, as we will see in the next chapter.

The Our Father is primarily a prayer for disciples. Every line is about disciples forgetting their own desires and plans for their lives and desiring only what God wills. In that sense it is a dangerous prayer for anyone who prays it.

Far too often the Our Father is misused: as prayer-stuffing, as a liturgical measure of time ("Pause for the length of an Our Father"), or as a penance after confession ("For your penance, say one Our Father and one Hail Mary").

People in the early church were still aware of how precious an Our Father is. Only at the completion of the catechumenate was it "handed over"; that is, candidates for baptism were first introduced to the Our Father shortly before their baptism. This was called the *traditio orationis*. After baptism they were then permitted, for the first time, to recite the Our Father in the festal Mass, together with the whole congregation. Just as catechumens were solemnly presented with the Creed, so also they solemnly received the Our Father.

For us, the Our Father has often become routine. It is worn out. Its words and phrases are as blurred as a foggy landscape. "Hallowed be your name," "Your will be done"—it has all become vague. But on the lips of Jesus and in the ears of the disciples the Our Father had clear, sharply defined contours.

Now, to make those contours visible again, we will first say something about the form of the Our Father. The form of a text is never accidental. It is related to the subject, to what it is about. Here are five observations about the form of the Our Father:

*1. The Our Father is pure petition.*

It is universally accepted today and needs no further proof that the doxology "for the kingdom and the power and the glory are yours, now and forever" was only secondarily added to the Our Father. The oldest manuscripts do not yet contain a doxology. It probably comes from a time when the Our Father had become part of the eucharistic celebration. The original Our Father was nothing but petition.

Why didn't Jesus teach his disciples a doxology, a prayer of praise? Or a prayer like the beginning of the Jewish Eighteen Benedictions, the *Tefillah*? The *Tefillah* opens with:

> Blessed are you, O Lord our God and God of
> our fathers, the God of Abraham, the God of
> Isaac and the God of Jacob, the great, mighty
> and revered God, the Most High God who
> bestows lovingkindnesses, the creator of all
> things, who remembers the good deeds of the
> patriarchs and in love will bring a redeemer to
> their children's children for his name's sake. O
> king, helper, savior and shield. Blessed are you,
> O Lord, the shield of Abraham.

So why did Jesus not teach his disciples a prayer
that was at least framed by praise, as is Israel's daily
prayer? There is only *one* plausible explanation: the
urgent crisis and need of the people of God. The Our
Father is like a cry, begging that God will intervene.
Obviously, Jesus knew every kind of prayer, if only
from the Psalter. He knew praise, thanksgiving, lament. But *this* prayer, the one he gave his disciples
as their own proper prayer because it deals with the
reign of God now breaking forth, is pure petition.

### 2. The Our Father is a very short prayer.

Even in translation it is very brief. By way of comparison, the Jewish *Tefillah* has more than 1,300 words
in the translation cited above, whereas the Our Father
(without the doxology) contains only fifty-five words

in English. The Semitic version was even shorter. Without doxology and conclusion, Luke's version (which is probably closer to the oldest form of the Our Father) contains only twenty-three words in a back-translation into Hebrew. Why so short? The answer is in Matthew 6:7-8, a Jesus saying that Matthew quotes immediately before the Our Father:

> When you are praying, do not heap up empty phrases as the Gentiles do; for they think that they will be heard because of their many words. Do not be like them, for your Father knows what you need before you ask him.

*3. The Our Father gets right to the point.*

For comparison, let us look again at the beginning of the Eighteen Benedictions:

> Blessed are you, O Lord our God and God of our fathers, the God of Abraham, the God of Isaac and the God of Jacob, the great, mighty and revered God, the Most High God who bestows lovingkindnesses, the creator of all things, who remembers the good deeds of the patriarchs and in love will bring a redeemer to their children's children for his name's sake. O king, helper, savior and shield. Blessed are you, O Lord, the shield of Abraham.

That is a slow approach. The one praying is moved and sustained by the history of Israel. Something needs to be said about it first of all, at least by way of reference. Only then is there room for petitions. It probably suggests that it would be impolite to go charging through God's door with urgent requests. The distant background may even be an element of court ceremony. Before petitioners reached the king's throne room they would first be led through a number of anterooms. Then they had to walk the whole length of the throne room itself in order at last to arrive at the royal throne. They would prostrate themselves there. At a signal from a royal official they could speak, but still they had to be careful about choosing the proper address. Only after completing the long ritual could they finally present their petitions.

It would be worthwhile at this point to make a tour of ancient Near Eastern prayers, with their highly ritualized appeals to the deity who was being invoked on each occasion. Such a comparison would reveal all the more sharply the difference between them and the address to God in the Our Father, as well as in the Jewish tradition of prayer. Thus one of the Akkadian prayers of "raising the hands" begins:

> God of Heaven and Earth, Firstborn of Anu,
> Dispenser of Kingship, Chief Executive of the

Assembly of the Gods, Father of Gods and Men,
Granter of Agriculture, Lord of the Airspace . . .

One senses that the forms of address had to be precise; otherwise the god might not listen. And the titles are listed so that the particular god being addressed would really listen. It is not at all a simple matter to speak to him without making a mistake. Correct language and competence in praying are required. Above all, one must know the deity's proper name.

Nothing of the kind in the Our Father! *Abba*—that is the only address. It is familial. The communicative situation of the Our Father is not that of a king's court ceremonial but family intimacy—more precisely, that of Jesus' "new family." In a family, people speak to one another directly, without ceremony and without pretense. When things are right in the family, people speak to each other with profound mutual understanding.

That is why the Our Father gets to the point so directly and why it is so brief: it is a prayer for the new family of disciples. That is why it lacks even a hint of solemnity or a whisper of court ceremony.

Certainly that does not mean that all Jewish prayers are long and wordy. Judaism also has brief, concise prayer texts. For example, the Jewish *Kaddish* can be compared to the Our Father. One early version reads:

> Exalted and hallowed be God's great name in the world which God created, according to plan. May God's majesty be revealed in the days of our lifetime and in the life of all Israel—speedily, imminently, to which we say Amen. Blessed be God's great name to all eternity.

As we can see right away, this prayer agrees in many ways with the Our Father, not only formally but in its content. The first petition in the *Kaddish* is also for the hallowing of God's name, and the second asks for the coming of the reign of God. To that extent the proximity of the Our Father to the *Kaddish* leaps out at us immediately.

Still, we must also note the differences. The *Kaddish* is not pure petition. At least in the version given here it is combined with praise: "Blessed be God's great name to all eternity." It is possible that the praise was, in fact, the core and origin of this Jewish prayer (cp. Ps 113:2; Dan 2:20). And something else should be noted: in its original function the *Kaddish* was not a prayer that stood alone; it was a concluding formula, an ending. It was created for recitation at the end of the Scripture reading in synagogal worship. So it remains true that the Our Father, as a prayer complete in itself, is highly unusual in its compactness.

### 4. God's interest comes first.

The Our Father is clearly divided into two parts. In Matthew's version each of the two sections contains three (or four) petitions. First there are three "thou" askings:

> (1) Hallowed be your name
> (2) Your kingdom come
> (3) Your will be done

Then (depending on how one counts them) follow three or four "we" petitions:

> (4) Give us today our daily bread
> (5) Forgive us our trespasses
> (6) Lead us not into temptation
> (7) but deliver us from evil

Thus the two-part division of the prayer is very clear. When the Our Father is translated back into Hebrew it becomes even more obvious because of its rhythm and rhyme. The first part is marked by the end-rhyme *-eka*; the second by the end-rhyme *-enu*.

The first part of the Our Father is concerned with the name, reign, and will of God. We could say it is about God's concerns. The disciples' interests—concerning food, their sinfulness, the crisis of their temptations—only come into play in the second part. Thus the structure of the Our Father matches Jesus' admonition exactly: "But strive first for the kingdom of God and his righteousness, and all these things will be given to you as well" (Matt 6:33).

Those who make God's concerns entirely their own will find that God cares for them as well.

## 5. God acts through people.

Another observation, merely formal to begin with, is in order: the first three petitions are oddly constructed: "Hallowed be your name; your kingdom come; your will be done." We are so familiar with the phrasing of the Our Father that we no longer notice how unusual these constructions are. No one talks that way in real life. No one says: "May the hallway be swept. . . . May cleanliness come."

Ordinarily we talk in such a way that it is clear who is supposed to be acting, who is the active subject. We don't say, "May the hallway be swept," but "Please sweep the hallway!" Why doesn't the Our Father simply say "Father, hallow your name, bring your reign into being, accomplish what you will"? Many interpreters of the Our Father assert that the indirectness of the construction is a matter of politeness. You don't talk to God so boldly. Besides, the word "God" is to be avoided, and that is accomplished through the so-called *passivum divinum*. "Hallowed be your name," for example, is a *passivum divinum*, an indirect expression ensuring that God is not addressed too baldly: thus not "God, hallow your name," but "Hallowed be your name."

But this politeness theory cannot apply, at least not to the Our Father, because as we have already seen, the Our Father avoids any kind of court ceremonial. It speaks in family terms, directly and without any fancy words. Besides, the second part of the Our Father is very direct:

> Give us this day our daily bread!
> Forgive us our trespasses!
> Lead us not into temptation!
> Deliver us from evil!

These expressions in the second half are, without exception, petitions addressed directly to God. So the Our Father has no hesitation about talking directly to God without beating around the bush. Then why the indirect constructions in the first three petitions?

There can be only *one* reason: the indirect constructions, above all the passive in the first petition, leave the question of the active subject open. "Hallowed be your name." We can add "by you yourself," but just as well "by human beings." Both are possible; both are correct. And apparently Jesus intended that ambiguity. God is asked to hallow the divine name and bring the reign of God into being. God is to bring the divine will to fulfillment. That is first and most important. But at the same time the disciples are to hallow the name of God, and they too are to make space for the reign of God. They themselves are also to do the will of God.

So with the aid of language forms the first three petitions of the Our Father express a fundamental theological insight: God takes the initiative. God acts. Everything comes from God. And yet, because of the independence and freedom God wills for human beings, God can do nothing in the world unless there are people who are prepared to make God's will their own and thus make space for God to act.

For this reason there is a great deal of theology even in the *form* of the Our Father and thus, of course, in the seven petitions themselves. In the Our Father, Jesus summarized all that he wanted and hoped for.

# 2. The Original Situation

THE OUR FATHER is not a universal prayer. It has a clear *Sitz im Leben* (life situation), to use an expression from biblical scholarship. It is primarily a prayer for Jesus' group of disciples. That is especially clear in the fourth petition, the plea for daily bread. For that reason we need to discuss the fourth petition first. It sheds more light than any other part of the prayer on the original context in which the Our Father was located. And what was that? What are the "coordinates" within which Jesus' disciples pray the Our Father?

Jesus lived an irregular life, wandering through Israel, constantly on the move in order to announce the beginning of the reign of God everywhere in the land. The Twelve accompanied him, together with a larger group of disciples. His disciples *followed* him, which is to say that "following" Jesus originally had a literal significance: traveling with Jesus throughout the land and usually not knowing in the morning where the night would be spent. After all, "Foxes have holes, and birds of the air have nests; but the Son of Man has nowhere to lay his head" (Matt 8:20).

There were others who did not travel with Jesus through the land and yet were highly important for his mission of proclamation, namely, Jesus' local "followers": those he had healed, friends, supporters, sympathizers, and all those who could be called curious in a good sense. The new thing Jesus had begun in Israel needed such local adherents; it needed friends and helpers. After all, Jesus and his disciples deliberately traveled defenselessly and without means. Why?

For one thing, their weaponless state was intended to distinguish them from the armed Zealots who at that time were on the move everywhere in Israel, collecting followers as well as money and weapons for a revolt against Rome. If Jesus' disciples were not to be confused with the Zealots, they must not carry money and arms. But that meant that when they had been on the road all day they needed to find people to receive them into their houses at eventide. They needed people who would provide them with food and shelter for the night. All that is reflected in the mission discourses in the gospels, for example in Luke 10.

When the text says that the disciples are not to greet anyone on the road, that of course does not refer to a brief greeting exchanged with passersby. It refers, rather, to the kind of long conversation that is usual in the Near East when people encounter one another in lonesome places. In such cases people ask each other where they come from and who their relations are, exchange information about where water is to be found, and tell of recent attacks. Above all, they share the latest news. Those endless discussions, which absorbed as much of the day as television does now, were to be avoided by Jesus' disciples. The time is short, because the reign of God is pressing near.

> Go on your way. See, I am sending you out like lambs into the midst of wolves. Carry no purse, no bag, no sandals; and greet no one on the road. Whatever house you enter, first say, "Peace to this house!" And if anyone is there who shares in peace, your peace will rest on that person; but if not, it will return to you. Remain in the same house, eating and drinking whatever they provide, for the laborer deserves to be paid. (Luke 10:3-7)

Other passages in the mission discourses even forbid the disciples to carry bread for the journey (cp. Mark 6:8; Luke 9:3). At first glance it seems as if the disciples are supposed to fast as much as possible, living austerely and meagerly.

But that is *not* what is meant. These mission discourses are in no way about asceticism and a modest lifestyle. They are about the sharp distinction from the Zealots and thus about standing for peace and against violence and war.

In the Israel that Jesus wants to gather and place under the rule of God there must be no violence and no holy war. Eschatological Israel must be a place of peace. That is why, when the disciples are proclaiming the reign of God, they must not carry provisions or weapons. Jesus even explicitly forbids them to carry a staff with which they could defend themselves (Matt 10:10; Luke 9:3; softened in Mark 6:8). They are not even to wear sandals, which could enable them to run away over the stony ground. That too demonstrates their defenselessness.

But if they have no weapons or equipment, and above all no money, they need to find people who will receive them into their houses in the evening, give them bread to eat, and provide something for the following day. That is the reason for the bread petition in the Our Father!

There is something else besides: the disciples have left everything: house, family, means of making a

living. And with the family, which was, in fact, an ex-
tended family, they have also left the father who cared
and planned for the family. It was simply understood
as a matter of course that the head of household had
to plan and provide for his family. But in this sense
those who had abandoned their families no longer
had fathers. That is why Jesus teaches them in the
Our Father to address God as their *abba*, their loving
and caring father.

Thus the *abba* at the beginning of the Our Father is
in no way gratuitous: it precisely expresses the situation of the new family in which the disciples now
live. The disciples who follow Jesus have received
God as their father in an entirely new and radical
sense. God now cares for them just as their biological
fathers had previously done. They can trust in God
unconditionally.

However, that trust is not something magical, ir-
rational, and baseless. Trust in God as their new *abba*
has a real basis. Jesus' disciples can count on it that in
the evening, when they need a roof over their heads,
they will again and again find houses to receive them.

Jesus' disciples do, in fact, live in a "new family."
They have had to leave their old, natural families for
the sake of announcing the reign of God. But in their
place they have found a new family with "a hundred

brothers and sisters" (Mark 10:30)—not just the other
disciples, but also the friends, sympathizers, and silent helpers everywhere in the land, people they can
trust. All that is reflected in the Our Father, which
begins with the address *abba* and in its fourth petition
asks for daily bread.

"Daily" bread? At this point there is a difficult
problem for translators. *Ton arton hēmōn ton epiousion*,
the Greek text reads. The version commonly used in
English-speaking countries is "Give us this day our
daily bread!" But the word *epiousion* does not appear
in any of the surviving Greek literature except here
in the Our Father. We have to reconstruct what the
word meant.

Probably it referred to bread for the day to come,
which in Israel began at evening. In that case *epiousion*
would be derived from *epienai* (impending, coming).
The Acts of the Apostles regularly refers to the "coming (day)," using *epienai* (see Acts 7:26; 16:11; 20:15;
21:18). In that case Jesus' disciples would be asking
for bread for the evening or for the day to come.

So there is no provision for a long period of time,
no planning for the future. The end-time situation
is so acute, the current proclamation so urgent, that
no planning is possible. Jesus and his disciples do
not yet know, in the morning, where they will be at

nightfall. They constantly live in the now, and their view extends only to the next day.

Hence we can paraphrase the bread petition this way: "Let us encounter people today who will receive us into their houses and give us something to eat in the evening, so that our lives and our food can be ensured for one more day!" Nothing more is possible, nor is it necessary, because Jesus' disciples are surrounded and supported by God's parental care.

In this way their situation corresponds to that of Israel in the wilderness narratives of the Old Testament. With its exodus, Israel had abandoned the basis for existence provided by the Egyptian welfare state. It was to begin a new social order of mutual solidarity. In the exceptional situation of wilderness God nourished the people with manna, but the Israelites were not permitted to store it up. Except for the day before the Sabbath, they could gather only what they needed for a single day. Exodus 16:4 speaks of the "measure of the day on its day" (*debar yom beyomo*), that is, the ration for the *one* day. It may be that *epiousios* attempts to fashion an allusion to Exodus 16:4 in Greek.

But however the language may have developed, it would be hard to imagine that Jesus would have formulated a prayer for bread for *one* day without thinking of the story of the manna. He knew that his disciples, who were proclaiming the reign of God throughout the land "like lambs in the midst of wolves" were, like Israel in ages past, in a wilderness situation that was, in principle, simply impossible.

In addition, the Our Father corresponds to Jesus' admonition in Matthew 6:34. Here too he speaks of the one, single day; we need not concern ourselves about how it should be located on the calendar: "So do not worry about tomorrow, for tomorrow will bring worries of its own. Today's trouble is enough for today." As we have already seen, but should emphasize again: this kind of carefree attitude has nothing to do with being starry-eyed, naïve, other-worldly, and that is precisely because the group of disciples does not exist by itself. There are sympathizers scattered throughout the land who will put their houses at the disciples' disposal. Jesus' disciples are not alone. They have friends. They can count on a lot of other people across the land. Think, for example, of Lazarus in Bethany and his sisters, Mary and Martha (Luke 10:38-42; John 11:1-5), or of the unknown man who provided a well-furnished upper room for Jesus and his disciples to eat the Passover Seder (Mark 14:12-26).

The bread petition in the Our Father shows us that something new was happening in Israel. The disciples were sent out without resources or provisions. They trusted in their *abba* in heaven—and in the solidarity of those who supported them from their own homes. In that way they could apply their whole strength to the proclamation.

We see, then, that the bread petition in the Our Father is anything but innocuous. It does not ask for the maintenance of bourgeois comfort, not even for "bread for the world." In it Jesus' disciples pray that every day they will have as much as is necessary so that they will retain strength and freedom to preach.

Indirectly this petition is about a new form of society, a new family in which all help each other to enable the proclamation of the reign of God. The post-Easter community called this new form of solidarity *agapē*. The word *agapē* means that each thinks in terms of the other, that each asks what the other needs and helps accordingly. The goal of this communion in *agapē* is to make the apostolic work possible: to enable Jesus' community to proclaim the Gospel through its messengers.

Let me repeat: the Our Father is not benign and nonthreatening. Even the apparently obvious request for daily bread is not innocuous, because it presumes that one desires the new family of Jesus, that one wishes to live in the daily company of many brothers and sisters and in the effort it makes possible on behalf of the Gospel.

So the very interpretation of the fourth petition of the Our Father makes it clear that a close examination of the form and historical situation of a biblical text is not a luxury. Rather, it is an aid to a better under-standing of the text. Only then can we apply it to our own situation. Only then can we ask ourselves: are we living this text and what it wants to tell us?

That means, in the case of the bread petition: are we taking care that the New Testament community of many helpers and sympathizers exists in our congre-gations, again and again renewed, making it possible for others to be free to preach the Gospel?

# 3. The Surprising Address

*T*HE OUR FATHER, as Jesus taught it, began with the address "Father." This extremely brief form of address is retained in the Lukan version of the prayer. In all probability Matthew's version had already been liturgically expanded. There it reads: "Our Father in heaven." Naturally, any absolutely certain proofs of the oldest version of the text are impossible in such cases, but we must suppose that a prayer originally given by Jesus would have been expanded rather than abbreviated. Moreover, the extremely brief address in the Lukan version corresponds to the terse form of the Our Father.

I have already anticipated in the first two chapters that on the lips of Jesus the beginning of the Our Father must have been *abba*. In recent decades scholars have written at extraordinary length about this Aramaic *abba*. It seems that the word comes originally from intimate family life; however, *abba* is far removed from its origins in childish babble. We should by no means try to equate it with our "Papa" or "Daddy," as was asserted at one time.

Nevertheless, the word still contains tenderness and confidence within its meaning. Jesus dared this intimate address almost as if it were a matter of course. He could venture it on the basis of his relationship to his heavenly Father and at the same time because of the experience of the new family he had begun with his disciples. After all, the disciples had left their fathers and mothers for Jesus' sake. All they had left was their Father in heaven. This new situation still echoes in a rule of the young church directed against the rapidly rising claim to titles: "And call no one your father on earth, for you have one Father— the one in heaven" (Matt 23:9).

But how do we even know that the Our Father originally began with *abba*? The original texts of Matthew (6:9) and Luke (11:2) do not have *abba*, but the Greek form of "father." How can we be sure that Jesus did not simply choose to begin the Our Father with the Hebrew form *abinu* ("our Father")?

As odd as it seems at first glance, the beginning of the Lord's Prayer can be deduced from the letters of Paul, who writes in Romans 8:15: "you have received a spirit of adoption. When we cry, 'Abba! Father!'

it is that very Spirit bearing witness with our spirit that we are children of God." Similarly, Paul writes in Galatians 4:6: "God has sent the Spirit of his Son into our hearts, crying 'Abba! Father!'"

Why would Paul have used that foreign-sounding *abba* unless it was dear and precious to Christians at the time? They knew that it was Jesus' language. That is how he addressed his dear Father before he suffered (Mark 14:36). So the Our Father left its echo even in the letters of Paul. The original address to God in the Our Father was unforgettable.

What the first Christians found so incomprehensible and so precious—that they were permitted to address God as *abba*, "dear Father"—creates problems for us later Christians. Does it mean that God is a man? Ultimately even a patriarch? Don't we have to finally shatter this whole image of God from times past in order to get at the true image of God, emphasizing God's feminine features equally with the masculine? And not only in theological scholarship, but in our very language? Isn't our language still profoundly shaped by patriarchy, so that it continually creates patriarchal structures?

Such thoughts have long circulated in the United States and Canada, and they have become pervasive in Europe as well. It has been suggested for some time now that we should alternate "Our Father" with "Our Mother" when we pray. "Our Mother" has for quite a while been used in paraphrases of the Our Father. But because the shift is not easy to manage, some Protestant biblical scholars recently produced a *Bibel in gerechter Sprache* [Inclusive-Language Bible] in which Matthew's version of the Our Father no longer begins "Our Father, who art in heaven," but "You, O God, are our Father and Mother in heaven."

What has happened here? For the purpose of gender-neutral language the familiar, trusting address "Father" has become the cooler "God." And the liturgical expansion "in heaven," which is altogether the language of prayer, has become a lesson in feminism. Strictly speaking, it is no longer God who is addressed at the beginning of this new prayer; instead, those praying are instructed about how they ought to imagine God.

But that turns the beginning of the Our Father into its opposite. The direct address to the Father in heaven that Jesus spoke, trusting and free of all ceremony, now becomes a ceremony of feminist instruction. The rendering of the Lukan version is even worse. There, necessarily, "Father" becomes "O God!" because it seems that no one wanted to write "O Father, O Mother!" And the early Christians, who according to Romans 8:15 had received the Holy Spirit and by the strength of that Spirit cried "Abba! Father!" have now received a holy "spiritual power" and no longer cry "Abba" but "Thou origin of all life, be our protector!"

Thus the apparently just language does massive injustice to the text. We can in no way take it for granted that Jesus' address to the Father retained the idea of patriarchal structures. Jesus did not submit himself to his clan or allow his relatives to prescribe his way of living; he left his family behind (Mark 3:20-21, 31-35). And he promised his disciples that in the new family they would have a hundred brothers, sisters, and mothers—but *not* a hundred fathers (Mark 10:30).

It is true that the Old Testament often speaks of God's motherly characteristics and compares God to a mother (e.g., Isa 66:13). But it never describes God directly as a mother, and certainly it does not address God as "mother." Is there not a profound reason for that, namely, that in the Old Testament the relationship between God and God's people is seen by analogy with the relationship between man and woman? The people of God can be described as God's beloved, as God's bride (e.g., in Ezek 16). She has been chosen and wooed by God, and God has brought her home.

She is the one who listens and receives, though she is also faithless. Within such a metaphorical world, which is fundamental to the Bible, extending deeply into the New Testament (cp. only 2 Cor 11:2 and Eph 5:25-32), God must be referred to in masculine terms, no matter how much that is purely metaphorical and no matter how profoundly true it is that God's motherly features may not be omitted. Is it permissible simply to shatter the structure of this imagery?

But probably the distress of feminists is not the most profound problem that Christians today have with the "father" address in the Our Father. It may well be much more difficult for those who had no father or have experienced only a distorted image of fatherhood—the many, many children of the "fatherless society." Can they get any sense at all of what it means to confess God as father and to address God that way?

Here John 14:9 offers some help: "Whoever has seen me has seen the Father." This assures us that ultimately we can recognize God only when we look at Jesus. He is the icon of God. In connection with our discussion this means that, indeed, not everyone has a father, or the right kind of father. But everyone can have Jesus as a brother, look to him, learn from him, follow the same path as he does. Those who do that will learn, through Jesus, what it means to say that God is our father. They will gain God as their father through Jesus. In following Jesus they will arrive at the very place where the Spirit of God makes us daughters and sons of God and cries within us, with "sighs too deep for words" (Rom 8:26): "Abba! Father!"

Still, those who have the greatest problem with the "Father" address are the many for whom the image of the Father has altogether vanished in the midst of the unspeakable suffering of the world and the millions of murdered Jews. The Jewish poet Rose Ausländer (1901–1988) wrote of the *Shoah*:

> Our Father
> take back your name.
> We do not dare
> to be children
> who say "Father"
> with throttled voices,
> Lemon-yellow stars
> nailed to our foreheads.
> . . .
> Our Father,
> we give you back
> your name.
> Go on playing "father"
> in a childless,
> airless heaven.

There is no cheap answer we can give to this text, which is more a despairing cry and a lament than an accusation. The only answer could come if Christians really lived as children of God, and that means as brothers and sisters for the sake of others—above all for their Jewish sisters and brothers. Then the face of the Father would no longer be distorted.

# 4. The Gathering of the People of God

THE OUR FATHER can be a stumbling block—when Christians make it a religious performance with no consequences. Then people who refuse to accept such sham prayer get really annoyed, and their scorn is likely to be directed at the wrong target: the Our Father itself. In 1992 the artist Cosy Piéro posted a placard on the door of the Theatinerkirche in Munich with the following twist on the Our Father:

> Human that I am on earth,
> hallowed be my name,
> my kingdom come and
> may it be done through my own free will.
> I forgive my own guilt
> and that of my neighbor
> and release myself from all evil
> for that is my power and beauty
> for a short time.

Now the human being is at the center, consistently and logically put in place of God, holy as such, hopeful of his or her own proper kingdom. This person elevates her or his own will, forgives personal guilt, and pronounces release of the self from all evil.

This "Our Father" means to be honest. It revolts against an Our Father that is nothing but vague religious babble. It does not believe that Christians are really asking for what they say they are. Nor will Christians' "Our Father" be believed if it has no basis in a society that tries to match the words they speak in the Our Father. That basis, that ground, is made up of followers and disciples—surrounded by those who sustain and enable the disciples: in short, those who are the people of God in the New Testament sense.

What is so surprising, though, is that this people of God, without whom there can be no disciple-lifestyle, seems to be entirely absent from the Our Father. That is peculiar, and all the more so because it was taken for granted by Jews that one should pray for the people of God. The first example we may cite is the *Kaddish*, which prays explicitly for the hope "of the whole house of Israel." A second example is the *Tefillah*, the Eighteen Benedictions (*Shemoneh Esreh*). The seventh of those reads:

Look upon our affliction and plead our cause,
and redeem us speedily for Your name's sake;
for You are a mighty Redeemer. Blessed art
thou, O L–rd, the Redeemer of Israel.

The eighth petition follows with:

Heal us, O L–rd, and we shall be healed; save
us and we shall be saved; for You are our praise.
Grant a perfect healing to all our wounds; for
You, almighty King, are a faithful and merciful
Physician. Blessed art thou, O L–rd, who heals
the sick of Your people Israel.

Then in the fourteenth petition we read:

And to Jerusalem, Your city, return in mercy,
and dwell therein as You have spoken; rebuild
it soon in our days as an everlasting building, and speedily set up therein the throne of
David. Blessed art thou, O L–rd, who rebuilds
Jerusalem.

The seventeenth petition reads:

Accept, O L–rd our G–d, Your people Israel
and their prayer; restore the service to the
inner sanctuary of Your house; receive in love
and favor both the offerings of Israel and their

prayer; and may the worship of Your people Israel be ever acceptable unto You.

Finally, the eighteenth and last petition asks:

Grant peace, welfare, blessing, grace, loving-kindness and mercy unto us and unto all Israel, Your people. Bless us, O our Father, even all of us together, with the light of Your countenance; for by the light of Your countenance You have given us, O L–rd our G–d, the Torah of life, lovingkindness and righteousness, blessing, mercy, life and peace; and may it be good in Your sight to bless Your people Israel at all times and in every hour with thy peace. Blessed are You, O L–rd, who blesses Your people Israel with peace.

So the petitions are constantly about and on behalf of the people of God. That is taken for granted in Jewish theology. Many of the psalms end quite abruptly with a petition for Israel, e.g.:

Redeem Israel, O God, out of all its troubles.
    (Ps 25:22)
O save your people, and bless your heritage;
    be their shepherd, and carry them forever.
        (Ps 28:9)

> May the LORD give strength to his people!
> > May the LORD bless his people with peace!
> > > (Ps 29:11)
> Peace be upon Israel! (Pss 125:5; 128:6)

Why, then, does Israel, the people of God, not appear in the Our Father? But it does! It is only that we no longer recognize it because we spend so little time with the Bible. The very first petition in the Our Father, which we are discussing, is nothing other than a petition for the gathering and sanctification of the people of God.

"Hallowed be your name": This kind of language no longer speaks to us. It survived into the twentieth century, at least, in formulae like those taught to children preparing for confession: "I used the name of God irreverently." But the Bible means a great deal more when it speaks of "hallowing the divine name" than simply not using a word disrespectfully.

The background for the phrase "hallowing of the name" is the book of Ezekiel, especially chapters 20 and 36. Ezekiel speaks repeatedly of the holy name of God, and here (in Ezek 36:23) we find the only instance in the Hebrew Bible in which the statement that the divine name will be hallowed has God as the active subject.

In itself the hallowing of the name (*Kiddush HaShem*) is a theme found throughout the Old Testament and Jewish literature, but its subject is always the human being or the people Israel, and it is primarily about keeping the commandments. Compare, for example, the basic text, Leviticus 22:31-33 ("You shall not profane my holy name, that I may be sanctified among the people of Israel").

The statement that God hallows the divine name, on the other hand, leads us to Ezekiel. We need to examine the text of Ezekiel 36, which is undoubtedly the background to the first petition of the Our Father. It is God who is speaking:

> I scattered them among the nations, and they were dispersed through the countries; in accordance with their conduct and their deeds I judged them. But when they came to the nations, wherever they came, they profaned my holy name, in that it was said of them, "These are the people of the LORD, and yet they had to go out of his land." But I had concern for my holy name, which the house of Israel had profaned among the nations to which they came.
>
> Therefore say to the house of Israel, Thus says the Lord GOD: It is not for your sake, O house of Israel, that I am about to act, but for

the sake of my holy name, which you have profaned among the nations to which you came. I will sanctify my great name, which has been profaned among the nations, and which you have profaned among them; and the nations shall know that I am the LORD, says the Lord GOD, when through you I display my holiness before their eyes. I will take you from the nations, and gather you from all the countries, and bring you into your own land. I will sprinkle clean water upon you, and you shall be clean from all your uncleannesses, and from all your idols I will cleanse you. A new heart I will give you, and a new spirit I will put within you; and I will remove from your body the heart of stone and give you a heart of flesh. I will put my spirit within you, and make you follow my statutes and be careful to observe my ordinances. Then you shall live in the land that I gave to your ancestors; and you shall be my people, and I will be your God. (Ezek 36:19-28)

This text, which condenses and summarizes the whole book's expectation of salvation, contains six series of statements:

*First series:* Israel dwelt in the land God had given it, but it did not live according to the social order God had prescribed. It did not serve the God who had chosen it; it served other gods instead. In this way it despised the land and profaned the name of God. It filled the land with envy, hatred, and rivalry. In this way it spoiled the land and destroyed the beauty that was proper to the land it had been given.

*Second series:* God could not endure this profanation and contempt for the land; Israel had to be driven from the land and scattered among the nations. Why did God have to drive the people out? Today we reject such an image of God. Must God punish? Must God drive people away? We will get a better idea of what the Bible means if we reformulate these statements consistently in human terms: A society that constantly lives contrary to God's order of creation destroys itself. That is true in particular of the people of God, with its special calling on behalf of the other peoples. If it persistently acts contrary to its calling, it destroys the ground on which it stands. It destroys its basis. It exiles itself from its land and threatens its own existence.

*Third series:* Nevertheless, the scattering of Israel among the nations, brought about by Israel itself, did not make things better. They got worse, because that scattering meant that the name of God was profaned even more; now the whole world jeered at this people and its God. The pagan peoples said: what kind of miserable, powerless god is this YHWH? He is a god who does not take care of his people. He is a god without a people, a god without a land.

*Fourth series:* God had to put a stop to this making fun of the divine name. It was unendurable that the name of God should continue to be made a laughing-stock among the nations because of Israel's dispersion. Therefore God would act to hallow the divine name before all the nations. God's intervention was not something Israel had earned:

> It is not for your sake, O house of Israel, that I am about to act, but for the sake of my holy name, which you have profaned among the nations to which you came. (Ezek 36:22)

*Fifth series:* How did God put an end to that unbearable state of things? How did God hallow the divine name? God did so by gathering the people of God from its dispersion and leading it back into the land. God hallowed God's name by freeing the Israelites from their idols and giving them a new heart and a new spirit. God removed the hearts of stone from their breasts and gave them hearts of flesh. So it became possible for Israel to live according to God's social order.

*Sixth series:* At the moment when Israel lives again, as a renewed people, according to the will of God, the land itself is changed. Grain grows abundantly, the trees are laden with fruit. The wasteland becomes a paradise. The inhospitable cities become beautiful again. When all that happens, the nations will know who God is. Then God's name will be hallowed by them also, and the nations will give God glory:

> Then the nations that are left all around you shall know that I, the LORD, have rebuilt the ruined places, and replanted that which was desolate; I, the LORD, have spoken, and I will do it. (Ezek 36:35-36)

The first petition of the Our Father summarizes this whole text complex from Ezekiel in a single phrase. So when we pray "hallowed be your name," we ask God to

- accept the people of God,
- assemble that people from its dispersion,
- make it again to be one people,
- give it a new heart,
- fill it with holy Spirit.

In other words: in the first petition of the Our Father we beg that there may once more be a place in the world through which God's glory and honor may again be made visible—a place because of which

God's name can also be honored by the Gentiles and indeed can be called upon by them.

It is also true, however, that we do not encounter the people of God in the Our Father in the same way as in the Jewish Eighteen Benedictions. There is nothing here about the house of David. The city of Jerusalem is not mentioned. Nothing is said about Zion and the temple. That is because in Jesus' time all of that would have been easily misconstrued in political fashion, primarily because of the Zealot movement with which Jesus was constantly confronted, but also because of other people's ideas. For Jesus the only thing at stake is the honor of God, God's great name. The only honor and glory of God is God's people, but not understood in the sense of a nation-state; rather, this is the people Ezekiel has in mind. Hence the prayer is already open to the Pentecost experience of the community of disciples.

All that makes it clear that the petition in the Our Father in no way resembles a vague, indefinite, roundabout, indistinct phrase into which we can read just about anything. The first petition of the Our Father, which Jesus apparently regarded as the most important and urgent thing for which his disciples ought to pray, has a precise meaning, a clearly defined content: it is about the eschatological gathering and restoration of the people of God. That is how the name of God is to be hallowed.

But that also reveals the whole claim of the Our Father. Properly, it can be prayed only by those who long for the gathering of the scattered and divided people of God. Properly, only those may pray it who are prepared to work together, with all their strength, for the renewal of the people of God.

# 5. The Coming of God's Reign

*T*HE FIRST PETITION of the Our Father has a clearly defined background in Scripture: the theology of the book of Ezekiel. In a single brief sentence that first petition evokes an entire book before the eyes of those who pray it. Is the situation similar in the second petition?

In fact, that is the case. Here the background is found in another of the great prophets, namely, Daniel. In Daniel 7:13-14 royal rule over the whole earth is given to a "son of humanity" or "son of man" (NRSV: "human being"). What is special about Daniel 7:13-14 is that it speaks both of "coming" and of "royal rule/kingship." That "royal rule" or "reign" is precisely what Jesus is referring to when he speaks of the "reign of God" or "God's rule." The Greek word behind all of these various familiar translations is always *basileia*, in Hebrew *malkuth*. All that is background to the text:

> I saw one like a human being
>> coming with the clouds of heaven.
> And he came to the Ancient One
>> and was presented before him.
> To him was given dominion
>> and glory and kingship,
> that all peoples, nations, and languages
>> should serve him.
> His dominion is an everlasting dominion
>> that shall not pass away,
> and his kingship is one
>> that shall never be destroyed. (Dan 7:13-14)

This text appears frequently in the liturgy of churches that follow a lectionary: for example, in Year B on the last Sunday of the church year, the feast of Christ the King. But wherever the Daniel text is used in the liturgy it is divorced from its context, like a raisin picked out of a bun. This selective method makes a bland abstraction of the crucial concept of God's reign that is so central for Jesus.

This surgery performed on the text makes it impossible to understand what "reign" or "kingship" means in Daniel 7—just as impossible as it is to grasp who the "human being" or "son of man/humanity" is. So in what follows we will examine the whole context in Daniel 7:2-14. It will then be clear that for Daniel the "coming" that is so important in the second petition of the Our Father already meant the coming of God's reign—precisely because the "human being/ son of man" represents a *society*, and in fact a society to which God eternally gives the *basileia*, the rule, the kingship, the reign.

> I, Daniel, saw in my vision by night the four winds of heaven stirring up the great sea, and four great beasts came up out of the sea, different from one another. The first was like a lion and had eagles' wings. . . . Another beast appeared, a second one, that looked like a bear. It was raised up on one side, had three tusks in its mouth among its teeth and was told, "Arise, devour many bodies!" After this, as I watched, another appeared, like a leopard. The beast had four wings of a bird on its back and four heads; and dominion was given to it. After this I saw in the visions by night a fourth beast, terrifying and dreadful and exceedingly strong. It had great iron teeth and was devouring, breaking in pieces, and stamping what was left with its feet. It was different from all the beasts that preceded it, and it had ten horns. I was considering the horns, when another horn appeared, a little one coming up among them; to make room for it, three of the earlier horns were plucked up by

the roots. There were eyes like human eyes in
this horn, and a mouth speaking arrogantly.
As I watched,
thrones were set in place,
    and an Ancient One took his throne,
his clothing was white as snow,
    and the hair of his head like pure wool;
his throne was fiery flames,
    and its wheels were burning fire.
A stream of fire issued
        and flowed out from his presence.
A thousand thousands served him,
    and ten thousand times ten thousand stood
        attending him.
The court sat in judgment,
    and the books were opened.
I watched then because of the noise of the ar-
rogant words that the horn was speaking. And
as I watched, the beast was put to death, and
its body destroyed and given over to be burned
with fire. As for the rest of the beasts, their dominion was taken away. . . . As I watched in
the night visions,
    I saw one like a human being
        coming with the clouds of heaven.
    And he came to the Ancient One
        and was presented before him.
    To him was given dominion
        and glory and kingship,

    that all peoples, nations, and languages
        should serve him.
    His dominion is an everlasting dominion
        that shall not pass away,
    and his kingship is one
        that shall never be destroyed. (Dan 7:2-14)

We see right away that the text is coded so that the uninitiated cannot understand what it is about. If they could, the author might be in danger. The text was written in Israel at a time of great distress, and it was written for believing readers who could understand the coded language. So it has to be decoded.

Daniel is an alias for a theologian and prophet whose name we no longer know. He lived in the second century before Christ, under the rule of Antiochus III and Antiochus IV, the famous Syrian rulers. We know that Antiochus IV tried to Hellenize Israel and was supported in this by enlightened, liberal Jewish circles. We recall the Maccabees' struggle against the paganization of Israel. Antiochus IV reigned from 175 to 164 BCE. He plundered the Jerusalem temple and entered the holy of holies, which for law-observant Jews was a sacrilege. He established a cult of Zeus Olympios within the temple. Jews were forbidden their own cultic practices; they were not even allowed to observe the Sabbath. Antiochus had his subjects celebrate him as *Theos Epiphanes*, "God in Person." That is the immediate historical background for the book of Daniel and its eschatological hope.

Because this was a time when faith was in crisis, a time of persecution, the text says: it is night. The four winds are the four points of the compass, an image of the fact that this text is about the whole world. The issue is no longer Israel but the history of the world, a universal history.

The great sea that appears in the night visions is not a geographically locatable body of water. It is the world ocean, the primal sea, and thus an image of chaos. For ancient peoples the ocean was chaotic and perilous.

The four animals thus emerge out of chaos, and they themselves represent the chaos of society. We should not really speak of them as animals but only as beasts, for that is the intent of the text. The four beasts represent four great world empires; we might say they stand for four societies that appear in turn, each more bestial and evil than the one before it. Here, for the first time in human history, the state is interpreted and depicted as a beastly monster, a wild creature. As for the details of the four:

For the author of Daniel, the lion represents the Babylonian Empire. Babylon was as irresistible as a lion. Israel had not been able to defend itself against that mighty power. Babylon conquered Jerusalem and deported the elite of the people.

The second beast, the bear, is the empire of the Medes, which in the sequence presented in Daniel follows that of Babylon. The statement that the bear has three tusks means that the Medes subjugated three kingdoms.

The leopard, the third of the beasts, is the Persian Empire. We know from history that the Persians developed so much power that they even subjugated parts of Greece. The four wings represent the penetrating power and swiftness of the Persian armies.

Then the prophet sees the fourth beast, and here images almost escape him, so horrible is this creature. It is the world power that is most dangerous to Israel's faith: the Hellenistic empire of the Syrians, the Seleucids, a successor state to Alexander's empire. The ten horns are ten Hellenistic rulers; the last, the "little" horn, is Antiochus IV. This "little" horn will then grow up to heaven in Daniel 8:9-10 and will sweep a portion of the stars from heaven.

When the arrogance of the last horn has reached its apex there appears an Ancient One: God. The meaning is not that God is an old man but that God is eternal. God alone is sovereign over history, not these bestial world empires. What follows illustrates that truth:

A heavenly court convenes to judge all the world empires, especially the fourth beast. There now appears before this tribunal a fifth empire, a fifth society. Its symbol is the "Son of Man," which means "a human being." This fifth society is very carefully distinguished from the preceding four. It is no longer brutal or beastly; it is, finally, a *human* society, and therefore it is symbolized not by animals but by a human being.

We have to observe how sharply the text distinguishes at this point: the fifth society does not emerge from the chaos (ocean) but from heaven. It comes "with the clouds of heaven." The new, eschatological society thus descends from above. It is unachievable by humans. It is the gift of God. It is the end of all government by force.

And yet: even though this new society of God comes from above and cannot be created by humans, it does not float somewhere above the world. Despite its heavenly origin it is altogether earthly and worldly. It is the true eschatological Israel, for in the interpretation of the vision that follows it is identified with the "holy ones of the Most High." An interpreting angel says to Daniel:

> As for these four great beasts, four kings [= king-
> doms] shall arise out of the earth. But the holy
> ones of the Most High shall receive the king-
> dom and possess the kingdom forever—forever
> and ever. . . . The kingship and dominion and
> the greatness of the kingdoms under the whole
> heaven shall be given to the people of the holy
> ones of the Most High; their kingdom shall be
> an everlasting kingdom, and all dominions shall
> serve and obey them. (Dan 7:17-18, 27)

Thus as far as exegesis is concerned there is no way around it: the "human being" is here identified with the "people of the holy ones of the Most High," that is, with the longed-for, eschatological Israel. This people who are to come stand out from all the powers that have gone before them and in no way correspond to what the Hellenizing circles in Jerusalem so dearly desire. Hence the "human being/Son of Man" is a figure, an image of the true *basileia*, the royal reign of God. At the same time it is a figure of the true Israel that serves only God the Father. The two are inseparable.

Daniel 7 is an incredible interpretation of history. There had never been anything like it in the world before. This interpretation of history is intended to say that one world empire replaces another. The potentialities of the successive empires are more and more dreadful. The potential for violence in the world is constantly growing. But all these empires will be judged, dominion will be taken from them, and in part they will perish in blood and fire. Something new "is coming" to replace them: a realm, a rule, a reign that originates entirely with God.

This picture of history in Daniel 7 was available to Jesus; he knew it from Scripture; he was familiar with its full power and depth. When he spoke of the "coming" of the reign of God he adopted this interpretation of history. But at the same time he modified it. What is different for Jesus?

First of all, there is the timeline! In Daniel the five different societies succeed one another: first Babylon, then the Medes, then the Persians, then the Syrians, and only when the domination of all the world empires has been exhausted does the true kingdom come. Only then comes the rule of the Human Being, that is, God's new society that is altogether different from all societies before it. But for Jesus the reign of God is coming already *now*, in the midst of history, simultaneous with the still ongoing dominance of the world empires. Jesus said, in fact: "If it is by the finger of God that I cast out the demons, then the kingdom of God has come to you" (Luke 11:20).

And there is yet more difference between Jesus' idea and that of Daniel 7: the new society of the reign of God not only begins in the midst of the still existing world empires; it begins in indissoluble connection with a single one. Jesus speaks of himself as the "human being/Son of Man," so that now the phrase is no longer only a symbol for God's new society; it is at the same time a secret name for Jesus himself. He is the "Human One," the "Son of Man." He himself is the *basileia*.

Still, Jesus does not have his disciples pray, in the Our Father, that all the world may know that he is the "Son of Man" or son of God. Instead, he teaches them to pray for the coming of God's reign, of God's new society as promised in the book of Daniel. We should note that difference. We must never separate the person of Jesus, his divine mystery, from what he wanted and what he gave his life for: the coming of the reign of God. And that reign of God is not some nebulous construct. It is linked to the people of God who are to be gathered, to the eschatological Israel, to the "people of the holy ones of the Most High."

Finally, there is a third modification: in Daniel 7 the end of the vision states that "all peoples, nations, and languages should serve" the Human One. But Jesus said of himself: "The Son of Man came not to be served but to serve, and to give his life a ransom for many" (Mark 10:45). Here again Jesus goes beyond the proposal in Daniel 7. Jesus' lordship is based on his service, his self-surrender even unto death.

Despite the three modifications thus listed (the reign of God is coming in the present; it is inseparably linked to the person of Jesus; it comes to serve the world), Daniel 7 is for us the authoritative interpretation of world history. It remains true that all rule by violence will continually fail and will often be destroyed in bloody and fearful fashion. Even the legitimate, indispensable monopoly of violence in free, just societies is not yet the last word in history. In the midst of all of these structures of power, in the midst of righteous and unrighteous violence, the reign of God is growing, even today. It has its place in the people of God, in the church, in God's new society.

What a promise, and what a challenge to us! We may live already in this new beginning. God has already presented it to the world as gift. God's new society is given to us, in Daniel's metaphor, "from above." We cannot make the new thing by ourselves. We only have to accept it. And we can continually experience the humanity of this new thing. It is no longer beasts that are the measure of history but the Human One, the "Son of Man," forever, for all time.

Thus when the Our Father prays for the coming of God's reign, the background lies in Daniel 7 and its powerful historical vision of the coming of a new community that is stronger than all world empires, all the power and violence of the world. When we beg that God's reign may come we are calling for a silent revolution that will change the world—not sometime or other, but *now*.

It is so important that we do not expect the realm of which Jesus speaks, and that we as his disciples are to pray for, only in the world beyond or in the depths of our souls. That would be to distort Jesus' message about the reign of God. The reign of God is supposed to begin here and now. That is what Jesus preached. And the reign of God has a social shape. It is not an invisible thing; that, at least, we can learn from Daniel 7. Because it has a social shape, its proper place is the church. Our first duty is not to improve the society around us but to live the church as God's new society. That is also our best service to secular society.

This in turn intensifies and expands the alertness that the New Testament repeatedly demands of us (see, e.g., Mark 13:33-37) to a still higher degree. We do not really do justice to the Gospel if we restrict the object of our attention to the coming of the Human One at the end of the ages. We must also, and primarily, keep alert for the coming of the reign of God that is trying to happen right now, among us. Therefore we must constantly ask ourselves: where do we find the signs of the reign of God today? Where, in our days, are people being freed from their demons? Where in our cities are people turning to the Gospel? Where are the people of God being gathered today "from the four winds" (Mark 13:27)? Where is the church, where are its congregations shedding their connections to the state and going their own way, the way of new community? That, after all, was the promise of Daniel 7: a completely different kind of society with a different origin, a society that sets its hopes not on the state and its power but on the new thing God intends to create in the midst of the nations.

We can, in fact, summarize all of these questions in one: where, today, is the church taking a form that allows it to measure itself against the standard of the New Testament? More precisely: where is it taking the form with which it has been gifted since Easter and Pentecost? All our attention should be focused in that direction. Only when we long for a new church and constantly stretch ourselves out toward it are we expecting the Human One and the reign of God in a way that is adequate to the Bible.

If we pray in the Our Father for the coming of the reign of God, we are praying for the end of the world—that is, the end of our old world, with all the powers we have thus far served, and the beginning of the new world that God is offering us already today. "Your kingdom come" therefore implies a radical exchange of rulers. In that way also, the Our Father is a dangerous prayer.

# 6. The Realization of God's Plan

"*Y*OUR WILL BE DONE." This third petition of the Our Father is not present in Luke's version. We find it only in Matthew. For that reason there is a widespread opinion that the petition is not original but was added by Matthew or the tradition *before* Matthew in order to round off the first part of the Our Father.

There is, in fact, a good deal in favor of this argument. The simple "Father" with which the Lord's Prayer begins had been expanded to "Our Father in heaven" in Matthew's version. Luke simply has "Father." Likewise, the last petition in the Lord's Prayer may have been correspondingly augmented with "but deliver us from evil," a petition that is absent from Luke's version.

What could have been the reason for such additions? Is it that liturgical texts tend to expand rather than contract? The closing doxology, "For the kingdom, the power, and the glory are yours," was certainly added to the Lord's Prayer. The same is equally possible for all parts of the Our Father in Matthew's version that go beyond Luke's. From that point of view the third petition could also be secondary.

That is not, however, altogether certain. Both Matthew and Luke shortened their Markan model in many places. In antiquity, in fact, students of rhetoric were routinely assigned the exercise of efficiently condensing existing texts. It should not be exegetical dogma that texts always grow longer over time.

But in the larger picture it is really unimportant whether the third petition was part of the Our Father from the beginning. I am interpreting the Lord's Prayer as we have received it from Matthew and Luke, and in terms of the content, the third petition is an extraordinarily good match for the first two; together they make up an internal unit.

Besides this, we must always take into account that texts whose wording does not stem directly and word for word from Jesus still express very precisely what he intended. It is even possible that a so-called non-genuine saying of Jesus is closer to Jesus than a "genuine" one. This is the case when it *interprets* what Jesus was and willed at its depth. Every historical truth is *interpreted* reality. The desperate attempt to distinguish "genuine" sayings of Jesus from "community constructions," which occupied all too much of the attention of exegetes in the nineteenth and twentieth centuries, was futile, because the only community competent to interpret the person of Jesus is the church.

The crucial question, then, is not "did Jesus also formulate a third 'thou' petition when he taught the Our Father to his disciples, or does the first part of the Our Father contain only two petitions?" The question should instead be: what does this third petition mean? How does it fit within New Testament theology? What does "your will be done" really ask for?

At first glance that seems obvious. Everyone believes instinctively that she or he clearly knows what the will of God is. Talk about the will of God has been so common among Christians over the centuries that we no longer even think about it. The Old Testament, Judaism, and the whole Christian tradition speak about the will of God. The expression is so common that we almost lose sight of it altogether. Because it is such a matter of course we pretty much fail to notice how it absorbs the horizons of thought and imagination proper to every epoch.

So we had better take a closer look. The formula "do the will of God" appears elsewhere: in the Old Testament, in Judaism, and repeatedly in Matthew's gospel. For example, the Sermon on the Mount ends, at Matthew 7:21, with "Not everyone who says to me, 'Lord, Lord,' will enter the kingdom of heaven, but only the one who does the will of my Father in heaven." Here the will of God, which human beings are to do, clearly refers to the commandments. We find the formula in the same sense in Psalms 40:8[9]; 103:21; 143:10. In each case it is about the *commanding* will of God: God's order, commandment, or the sum of the commandments.

Thus it seems probable that we should interpret the third petition of the Our Father in the same sense, above all because of the added "on earth as it is in heaven." In that case the petition would mean: just as in heaven God's will is done to the utmost, namely, by the angels, so it ought to be done on earth by human beings. In that interpretation Psalm 103:19-21 would be decisive. There we read:

> The LORD has established his throne in the
>     heavens,
>     and his kingdom rules over all.
> Bless the LORD, O you his angels,
>     you mighty ones who do his bidding,
>     obedient to his spoken word.
> Bless the LORD, all his hosts,
>     his ministers that do his will.

This section of Psalm 103 even seems to prefigure the sequence of the second and third petitions of the Our Father: first it speaks of God's royal rule, then of the fulfilling of God's will. Apparently that was so reasonable that for centuries the third petition of the Our Father was explained in the sense of Psalm 103. For example, the great theologian John Chrysostom wrote in his interpretation of the Our Father:

> He bade us indeed long for the things to come, and hasten towards that sojourn; and, till that may be, even while we abide here, so long to be earnest in showing forth the same conversation as those above. For you must long, says He, for heaven, and the things in heaven; however, even before heaven, He has bidden us make the earth a heaven and do and say all things, even while we are continuing in it, as having our conversation there; insomuch that these too should be objects of our prayer to the Lord. For there is nothing to hinder our reaching the perfection of the powers above, because we inhabit the earth; but it is possible even while abiding here, to do all, as though already placed on high. What He says therefore is this: As there all things are done without hindrance, and the angels are not partly obedient and partly disobedient, but in all things yield and obey (for He says, "Mighty

in strength, performing His word" [Ps 103:20]);
so vouchsafe that we . . . may not do Your will
by halves, but perform all things as You will.
(John Chrysostom, "Homily 19 on Matthew")

This is undoubtedly a magnificent and moving theology, one that we ought to live. Many centuries later,
Matthias Claudius said the same, in simple and gentle
words:

Here I represent to myself heaven with the holy
angels, who do his will with joy, and no sorrow
reaches them, and they know not how to keep
themselves from love and happiness, but rejoice
day and night; and then I think if it were only
so on earth!

So are we clear about the third petition of the Our
Father? No, not in the least—because if we interpret
it in this sense the third petition does not fit with the
first two. As we saw, the first petition has Ezekiel 36
as its background, and there it is *God* who takes the
initiative and hallows the divine name. It is true that
Israel's participation in the hallowing of the name of
God is the goal, but the one who truly acts is God.

The same is true of the second petition: the one
who brings the reign of God and gives it is God, not
humans. That is absolutely clear in Daniel 7. Therefore

in the second petition as well it is God who takes the initiative. People are to receive the *basileia*, enter into it, cooperate with it, but they cannot bring it about. Here, again, it is properly God who acts.

Can it be, then, that the third petition, which combines with the first two to form a unit, can suddenly shift from the direction of the other two and make human beings the only ones who act—by doing the will of God? That is hard to understand. So we need to look around and see whether it can be true that God's will is only a will that *commands*, that is, the "order," the "commandment," the "law."

For the moment let us stay with Matthew's gospel, because it is especially there that "will of God" in the sense of "commandment" is certainly attested. But the question is: does the will of God in Matthew always refer to the commandments, the law? We may begin with the well-known scene in Matthew 12:46-50:

> While he was still speaking to the crowds, his mother and his brothers were standing outside, wanting to speak to him. Someone told him, "Look, your mother and your brothers are standing outside, wanting to speak to you." But to the one who had told him this, Jesus replied, "Who is my mother, and who are my brothers?" And pointing to his disciples, he said, "Here are

my mother and my brothers! For whoever does
the will of my Father in heaven is my brother
and sister and mother."

"Here are my mother and my brothers!" With these
words Jesus constitutes the "new family" in a posi-
tively juridical formula. The new family exists wherever the will of Jesus' heavenly Father is done. But
what, in this situation, is the Father's will? It is most
certainly not the fulfillment of the Torah. Jesus is by
no means denying that his relatives obey the Torah.
That is not at all what this scene is about.

As the Markan parallel shows, Jesus' relatives
wanted to take him home and put him under "house
arrest." Mark even says "to restrain him" (Mark 3:21).
So his relatives do not understand that Jesus must
now "go public" in Israel, that he has to proclaim the
reign of God, has to gather Israel. *That*, for Jesus, is the
Father's will. It is something that goes far beyond any
fulfillment of the Torah. Doing this will means being
one with the program of salvation, with God's plan
for history. Accordingly, we read in John's gospel:
"My food is to do the will of him who sent me and
to complete his work" (John 4:34).

So this is about the "work of God," what God
means to begin in Jesus, what God needs him for.

Correspondingly, Matthew 12 is about God's "will," God's intent, God's plan. Those who enter with Jesus into this plan of God will be his brothers, sisters, even his mother: they will be the new family of God.

Thus in the scene in Matthew 12:46-50 "the will of God" means more than the commandments. Much more comprehensively, it describes what God intends for the world, what God is now doing in Israel through Jesus. The case is similar in Matthew's Gethsemane scene (Matt 26:36-46), where Jesus says in prayer: "My Father, if this [cup] cannot pass unless I drink it, your will be done" (Matt 26:42). That is the third petition of the Our Father, word for word, and again it is about more than simply fulfilling the Torah. There is nothing in the Torah about dying in such a situation. This is about God's plan of salvation, which is not blind fate, or the world law of the Stoics, or the will of an implacable God. Such interpretations are a far cry from what is meant here by the will of God. It is God's plan for history that is meant to liberate the world, but the world resists it because it desires not God but itself.

That resistance to God will bring about Jesus' death. But God makes the death of Jesus the saving consummation of everything he had proclaimed. Thus the will of God is God's will for salvation, which creates redemption in the face of all human sin. Therefore here "may God's will be done" means more than fulfillment of the commandments; it means surrendering oneself to God's saving decree.

We encounter this deeper, broader, and history-shaping sense of the "will of God" elsewhere in the New Testament as well. As one further example, consider Ephesians 1:

> Blessed be the God and Father of our Lord Jesus Christ, who has blessed us in Christ with every spiritual blessing in the heavenly places, just as he chose us in Christ before the foundation of the world to be holy and blameless before him in love. He destined us for adoption as his children through Jesus Christ, according to the good pleasure of his will, to the praise of his glorious grace that he freely bestowed on us in the Beloved. In him we have redemption through his blood, the forgiveness of our trespasses, according to the riches of his grace that he lavished on us. With all wisdom and insight he has made known to us the mystery of his will, according to his good pleasure that he set forth in Christ, as a plan for the fullness of time, to gather up all things in him, things in heaven and things on earth. In Christ we have also obtained an inheritance, having been

destined according to the purpose of him who
accomplishes all things according to his counsel
and will. (Eph 1:3-11)

This solemn opening of the letter to the Ephesians
is one long acclamation of God's plan for history, conceived from all eternity. It derives from the love of
God. The goal of the divine plan is to bring about
the fullness of time. When that goal of creation has
been achieved, everything will be brought together
in Christ, the head. Christ himself, and the church
gathered through him, is the concrete shape of that
plan. In Christ the accomplishment, the *oikonomia* of
God's plan is already fulfilled, but in the world it is
not yet so. The church is the tool through which God
will bring the world and all creation into the blessing
for which God has destined them.

Thus in this great text from Ephesians, which
almost takes the form of a liturgical Preface at the
beginning of the letter, we find nothing other than
a paraphrase of what is meant by the "mystery of
God's will." The word "will" appears within a whole
spectrum of nearly synonymous words: "decision,"
"good pleasure," "will," "plan."

What is important for our consideration in this
case is that the divine will, as a plan for the salvation

of the world, has existed from all eternity in heaven. It is this plan of salvation, in heaven and therefore preexistent, that God is now putting into effect on earth through Christ.

This gives "on earth as it is in heaven" a surprising, new, and much more revealing significance. "Thy will be done on earth as it is in heaven" thus means: "Make your plan of salvation, which you conceived in heaven from all eternity, become reality now on earth!"

Certainly the third petition of the Our Father does not say "Implement your plan of salvation!" but "Your saving plan, your will, be done!" We now understand why the Our Father uses such indirect phrasing: the subject remains open in order that human beings may also become subjects. In other words: God is not named as the one who accomplishes the plan, so that human beings may be included as coworkers. To put it still another way: God accomplishes the divine plan for salvation on earth, but human beings are called to open themselves to it, make it their own. Hence the indirect formulation: "Your will, your plan of salvation, be done!"

So in the third petition of the Our Father we pray that God's plan, determined in heaven, may come about on earth exactly as God has envisaged it from eternity. The content of that plan, indeed, is nothing other than what was asked in the first two petitions: that the reign of God may dawn, that the people of God may be gathered and made holy so that all peoples may give honor to God.

Is there a background in Old Testament Scripture for the third petition also? In considering the first petition we came across the theology of the book of Ezekiel, and for the second we saw an application of the theology of the book of Daniel. Is the third petition also based on the theology of one of the great prophetic books of the Old Testament? In fact, it is.

The idea that God is making a reality of the divine plan, will, decree for salvation in the world now is the deepest center of the second part of the book of Isaiah. Among all the prophets, only Isaiah speaks of the realization of God's will or the accomplishment of God's plan. There we read:

> [I say], "My purpose shall stand,
>     and I will fulfill my intention,"
> calling a bird of prey from the east,
>     the man for my purpose from a far country.
> I have spoken, and I will bring it to pass;
>     I have planned, and I will do it. (Isa 46:10-11)

The "bird of prey" is Cyrus, the Persian emperor who brought back the exiled Israelites from Babylon; hence this is about immediate expectation—an expectation regarding God's action in history. The "purpose" referred to here is God's decree, what God has "planned" and intends to "do." The end of this second part of the book of Isaiah will say:

> For as the rain and the snow come down from heaven,
> and do not return there until they have watered the earth,
> making it bring forth and sprout,
> giving seed to the sower and bread to the eater,
> so shall my word be that goes out from my mouth;
> it shall not return to me empty,
> but it shall accomplish that which I purpose,
> and succeed in the thing for which I sent it.
> (Isa 55:10-11)

The word of God, behind which stand the divine will and plan, is here compared to rain and snow that *come down from heaven* to earth. The plan of God will achieve its end. No one can destroy it.

If these observations are correct, then behind the first three petitions of the Our Father stand three of the great prophets of Israel: Ezekiel, Daniel, and Isaiah. Is that accidental or can we detect here one of Jesus' great mysteries? Jesus lived entirely on the basis of Scripture, though he was not a scribe. He understood Scripture at its full depth and took it at its word.

Is the third petition of the Our Father understood throughout the church in the sense I have described? Hardly. When we search our prayerbooks, or many pious explanations of the Our Father, we will find that the third petition is mainly interpreted purely in terms of *answer to prayer*, or of *Christian surrender* to what the individual may encounter. Many prayer texts urge us to those things, and we are almost instinctively inclined that way.

For example: a faithful Christian falls seriously ill. The doctors cannot help her. The patient says "That is my fate," or even "This is my mortal illness." First the sufferer resists, then surrenders and finds deep consolation in the idea that this is not blind fate; it is the will of God.

If we page through the prayers and hymns in our prayerbooks and hymnals we will find that the connotations of "will of God" are mainly sickness, need, suffering, misfortune, death—primarily the suffering and death of individuals. Obviously, that is all somehow right. God's plan for history is certainly about our personal stories and also the fears that reign in our lives. But in the Bible the "will of God" is above all God's "good pleasure," what God has desired from all eternity, what God constantly wishes and longs for. The will of God is what gives God joy and pleasure.

The will of God as expression of the great world-wide divine plan for history, as the letter to the Ephesians formulates it, appears all too rarely in our view. Hence it is improbable that our congregations really understand what we are praying for in the third petition of the Our Father. It is about God's great plan for the world, the people of God, the coming of God's reign.

Still, that third petition is dangerous, no matter whether one prays it more intensively in view of the world or of one's own self. Like the first two, it begs that God will intervene now, that God will be master and we will let God be God, that God will reassemble the people of God and make them holy so that salvation may come to earth through this people. That is God's plan, God's will, and whoever prays the Our Father enters into that will. That sort of thing changes one's life. Otherwise, praying the third petition of the Our Father is empty talk.

The first three petitions in the Our Father attempt to think entirely from God's point of view: that God's name be hallowed, that God's reign may come, that God's plan for the world may be realized. The petitions that follow, on the other hand, speak entirely from the point of view of the disciples: that they may find food and shelter for the night, that God may forgive their sins, and that God may preserve them from falling prey to temptation. We could also say that the first part of the Lord's Prayer speaks of God's concerns and the second part of those of the disciples.

But when we put it that way it immediately becomes clear that the two are intimately connected: God's care for the world is to be the disciples' concern, and the disciples' worry about their existence is something that has long been part of God's care for creation. If we look closely we see that the petitions in the second part of the Our Father are by no means private. They are about existence in the community of disciples, about the problems that arise precisely when people try to live, without reservation, for the sake of the reign of God. The interpretation of the bread petition already showed us that.

Early in this book we spoke at length about the fourth petition that begins the second part of the Our Father. So now we may proceed immediately to examine the petition for the forgiveness of sins.

# 7. Forgiveness of Sins

*I*N LUKE the fifth petition of the Our Father reads:

> And forgive us our sins,
>> for we ourselves forgive everyone indebted
>> to us. (Luke 11:4)

In Matthew's version it reads:

> And forgive us our debts,
>> as we also have forgiven our debtors.
>> (Matt 6:12)

We can see right away that the English forms familiar to us are a combination of Luke and Matthew:

> And forgive us our trespasses (or: forgive us
>> our debts)
>> as we forgive those who trespass against us
>> (or: as we forgive our debtors).

"Forgive us our trespasses/debts" draws on Matthew, while the present tense in "as we forgive" relies on Luke. Matthew has past tense here: the disciples have *already* forgiven their debtors all the indebtedness of sin; consequently, God can also forgive their sins. I will come back to this Matthean timeline, "forgive us—we ourselves have forgiven."

The fifth petition of the Our Father also can only be really understood if we see it as the prayer of the new family around Jesus, for it is there that forgiveness acquires special urgency—there, where believers allow themselves to be gathered into a new togetherness for the sake of the reign of God. There all the walls each individual has built around himself or herself are broken down. Nothing of one's identity remains hidden. It becomes directly evident that each is endlessly indebted to the other. There is no other way to understand Peter's shocked question in Matthew 18:21-22: " 'Lord, if another member of the church [lit.: brother] sins against me, how often should I forgive? As many as seven times?' Jesus said to him, 'Not seven times, but, I tell you, seventy-seven times.' "

Obviously, "seventy-seven times" is an Eastern expression (see Gen 4:24). It means "always, without limit!" The context shows that the NRSV is right to interpret "brother" as meaning "another member of the church." Matthew 18 is a careful composition entirely about life in community. It begins with the disciples quarreling about rank, then warns about leading disciples astray, and finally speaks of the shepherd's care for the lost and responsibility for fellow community members. Then comes Peter's question about how often he must forgive, after which the chapter ends with the parable of the pitiless debtor, a chilling deterrent example for those in the community who refuse to forgive.

The whole chapter shows that forgiveness is part of the life-breath of the community of disciples. There must be unconditional forgiveness at all times and everywhere—if only because God also continually forgives. This unremitting will to forgive reaches its limits only when a member of the community does not accept the counsel of the others and so places herself or himself outside the bounds of forgiveness (Matt 18:15-17).

But is the readiness to forgive spoken of in the Our Father demanded only of Jesus' disciples? Is it not also asked of Jesus' local friends and sympathizers who live in their homes here and there? To put it another way: is it not demanded of the whole people of God for whom Jesus lived and whom he desired to gather? The question is important because it is appropriate for resolving the problem of the addressees of the Our Father that I spoke of at the beginning of the book.

Let me, therefore, once again refer to a concrete text. It will show that the readiness to forgive that Jesus demands is asked not only of his disciples but of every member of the people of God. At the same time this text will cast more light on what it means to forgive. Matthew 5:23-24, a part of the Sermon on the Mount, says: "So when you are offering your gift at the altar, if you remember that your brother or sister has something against you, leave your gift there before the altar and go; first be reconciled to your brother or sister, and then come and offer your gift."

Here, then, is someone who wishes to honor God by making a pilgrimage to the temple. If the person is a Galilean, she or he will have been on the dusty and stony roads for several days. Now the pilgrim has arrived in Jerusalem, and we watch him or her bringing a gift to the altar.

That is the background situation, familiar to every one of the listeners at the time. Each of them felt included when Jesus continued: it may be that you are already in the process of presenting your sacrificial gift when suddenly you realize: "There is someone in my village, maybe in my own family, who has a complaint against me." If that happens, Jesus says, you are to leave your gift before the altar, return home, and be reconciled with your sister or brother. Then come back to the temple and make sacrifice.

What is remarkable in the whole process is, first of all, that Jesus does not say explicitly that the one with whom the person making the offering ought to be concerned is a disciple or follower of Jesus. In this case the word "brother [or sister]" leaves everything open. It may simply refer to your fellow man or woman within the people of God.

It is also notable that Jesus says nothing against the temple here. He apparently sees it as a matter of course that Jews from the motherland and from the Diaspora make pilgrimage to the temple in Jerusalem, that they give money to the temple, and that they purchase sacrificial animals and present them, take part in worship at the temple, and so give honor to God. What is more important to him, however, is that the members of the people of God should live in harmony with one another, in mutual forgiveness. If they do not, there is no sense in visiting the temple or making sacrifices. Jesus then continues immediately with a reference to the prophets' critique of cultic worship, for example, the words of God in Amos 5:

> I hate, I despise your festivals,
>    and I take no delight in your solemn
>       assemblies.
> Even though you offer me your burnt
>    offerings and grain offerings,
>  I will not accept them;
> and the offerings of well-being of your fatted
>    animals
>  I will not look upon.
> Take away from me the noise of your songs;
>  I will not listen to the melody of your harps.
> But let justice roll down like waters,
>    and righteousness like an ever-flowing
>       stream. (Amos 5:21-24)

If the social relationships within the people of God are out of line, the glory of the temple and the beauty of its liturgical worship are nothing but a farce. The prophets insist on this again and again. For members of God's people to live unreconciled alongside one another is as unacceptable to Jesus as social injustice. People who live together in unanimity and reconciliation are, for him, the indispensable precondition for every form of worship.

Finally, it is worth noting how Jesus sets the scene for the example he gives. He does not say, "When you are offering your gift at the altar, if you remember that you have insulted or angered your brother or sister, leave your gift there before the altar and go and ask your brother or sister to forgive you." Instead, he says: "if you remember that your brother or sister has something against you." Jesus is not interested in the identity of the guilty party; he deliberately leaves that question open. It is entirely possible that it is not the person in the temple who is at fault in the dispute but the one back home. Even so, the one in the temple must do everything possible to bring about reconciliation. She or he may not leave things as they are and most certainly must not say: "So-and-so started it, and so will have to be the one to begin restoring peace. That one will have to come and apologize to me. Then we can see what happens."

Those who think that way are being guided by bourgeois morality, not by the Gospel. Jesus is convinced that quarrels and enmities are so impossible within the people of God that an immediate attempt must be made to put an end to them, whether a particular individual is at fault or not. As long as one has not personally done everything possible to reconcile with the other there is no sense in going to worship. Such worship, Jesus says, is an abomination before God. But God rejoices in people who make peace, pursue it, and seek reconciliation.

Jesus' idea of reconciliation makes clear the difference between mere religion and Christian faith: every religion includes sacrifices brought to the gods, as well as feasts, pilgrimages, sanctuaries, holy water, altars, liturgy, prayer, ritual, fasting, almsgiving—such things are essential components of religion, and religion is universal.

But it is characteristic of the faith of the people of God that it says with incorruptible sober-mindedness: all prayer, all sacrificial practice, all worship is useless if it does not create a new common life. In worship God is reconciled to us and so takes the initiative; therefore we too must be reconciled, and we must take the initiative toward reconciliation as God does.

That, however, seems to contradict Matthew's version of the Our Father when it reads "forgive us our debts as we also have forgiven our debtors." But the problem resolves itself immediately when we consider the sequence in Matthew 5:23-24: someone intends to bring an offering to Jerusalem, visiting the place where glory is given to God, the temple. But this person may not bring the gift to the altar unless she or he has previously been reconciled with a fellow believer back home. Having forgiven the debtor everything, and having returned to Jerusalem, this person also receives full forgiveness from God. Reconciliation with the brother or sister in faith is the precondition for worship in the temple, and yet God has long since established this worship service as the enduring place for the giving of forgiveness. God took the initiative long ago.

Something analogous is true of Christian worship. The Our Father took its place there very early, being recited before reception of the Eucharist. The worship service has already begun before one approaches the temple and even before the Mass begins. It encompasses all of life—and not only encompasses it but changes it and shifts every horizon. The one who wants to sacrifice hurries back to create reconciliation, running her legs off to reach the opponent, pursuing him without knowing whether the offer will encounter an open heart: she herself becomes the sacrifice.

Suddenly we behold the way of Jesus and the sacrifice of his life behind Matthew 5:23-24. Jesus ran himself ragged for the sake of the people of God in order to create reconciliation, and his reward was to be crucified. From his death, however, arose the Easter communities, the enduring place of reconciliation.

But now to return to our initial question: it is probably clear by now that "forgive us our debts as we also have forgiven our debtors" is something that can be said not only by the disciples who are Jesus' immediate companions. As Matthew 5:23-24 shows, it applies to all members of the people of God. On the other hand, like the whole of the Our Father, it is first and primarily for the disciples who are the nerve-center of the eschatological Israel that is to be gathered again. Therefore we have to maintain the tension that constantly reveals itself: the Our Father is the disciples' prayer, formulated by Jesus for their very specific situation, and yet it is the prayer of all those in Israel who join in what is now happening through Jesus.

# 8. Protection in the Time of Testing

WE COME NOW to the sixth petition, probably the last in the Our Father as Jesus taught it (cp. Luke 11:4). If we suppose it is the last, the Our Father appears to be like a musical composition that ends with a dissonance, or a dramatic text closing with a loud cry: "Lead us not into temptation!" That is truly an appeal for help.

Even if a closing praise was very soon added, through all the centuries people at prayer have had their difficulties with this petition. Can God really tempt a person? The letter of James already contended with that problem:

> Blessed is anyone who endures temptation. Such a one has stood the test and will receive the crown of life that the Lord has promised to those who love him. No one, when tempted, should say, "I am being tempted by God"; for

> God cannot be tempted by evil and he himself
> tempts no one. But one is tempted by one's own
> desire, being lured and enticed by it; then, when
> that desire has conceived, it gives birth to sin,
> and that sin, when it is fully grown, gives birth
> to death. (Jas 1:12-15)

The connections to the Our Father are obvious. The author of the letter of James rejects a wrong understanding of the sixth petition: God tempts no one to evil. God simply cannot do that, for that would mean that God wills evil. No, people are spurred by their own desires.

All that is undoubtedly correct; still, James does not quite do justice to the biblical language in depth. But such problems with understanding had already begun in the Old Testament itself. In Sirach 15:11-13 we read:

> Do not say, "It was the Lord's doing that I fell
>     away";
>     for he does not do what he hates.
> Do not say, "It was he who led me astray";
>     for he has no need of the sinful.
> The Lord hates all abominations;
>     such things are not loved by those who
>         fear him [i.e., he does not let it happen
>         to those who fear him].

Thus on the margins of the Old Testament an "enlightened" theology begins to wrestle with the problem of whether God can tempt people to do evil. The early beginnings of the contention are connected with the language and thought patterns of older biblical texts, which see no problem in regarding God as the ultimate cause of everything in the world. Only in that way was it possible to refute belief in the working of foreign gods and powers. In the book of Isaiah, God promises favor to Cyrus:

> so that they may know, from the rising of the
> > sun
> > and from the west, that there is no one
> > > besides me;
> > I am the LORD, and there is no other.
> I form light and create darkness,
> > I make weal and create woe;
> > I the LORD do all these things. (Isa 45:6-7)

The problems with this kind of biblical language continue today. Catholic bishops have been petitioned for some time now to see to it that the sixth petition in the Our Father is translated differently. Otherwise, the text is continually misunderstood. Two alternatives are most often suggested:

> Do not let us fall into temptation!

and

> Do not permit us to fall into temptation!

But these suggestions are questionable, because the Greek text does not speak simply of allowing something to happen. It speaks of God's direct action: "Lead us not into temptation!" That corresponds exactly to the neighboring clauses. The second part of the Our Father always speaks of God acting directly:

> Give us our bread!
> Forgive us our trespasses!
> Lead us not into temptation!
> Deliver us from evil!

God is always the one who acts. We can only conclude that, for the Our Father, divine initiative is supremely important. This does not exclude human action, but God's action has an indispensable weight. Consequently, we should exercise the utmost caution in weakening precisely this aspect. So instead of hastily whitewashing the text, we should ask again: can God lead people into temptation? We find a first answer in the familiar story of the sacrifice of Isaac. Genesis 22:1 introduces it this way: "After these things God tested Abraham." "Tested" reflects exactly what the Hebrew text means to say. The Septuagint, the Greek translation of the Old Testament, reads *epeirazen*, which is the verb form of the very noun used in the sixth petition of the Our Father: *peirasmos*. We can see from this that in the Bible "temptation" or "testing" does not necessarily mean "temptation/testing" to do evil. Instead, in this instance God leads Abraham into a situation in which he must decide *against* God and thus for evil, or *for* God and thus for the good.

This is reflected in the sixth Our Father petition in that it does not say "do not test us" but rather "lead us not into temptation." The function verb, "lead," ensures that, as in the case of Abraham, God is the one who acts, but it also makes room for the noun "temptation," and the sequence "function verb, noun" leaves open the question of who is the tempter.

This distinction is confirmed by the way Jesus' temptation is depicted in the gospels. In Mark's version the crucial sentence is "And the Spirit immediately [after his baptism] drove him out into the wilderness. He was in the wilderness forty days, tempted by Satan" (Mark 1:12-13). The Holy Spirit, which had descended at Jesus' baptism, thus drives him into the wilderness—a space in which Jesus must repeat Israel's wilderness experience, a place where he is exposed to temptation by the Opponent, the Satan. God does not test Jesus and most certainly does not tempt him to do wrong. But God leads Jesus into a situation in which he is tested by Satan. Matthew states it even more clearly: "Then Jesus was led up by the Spirit into the wilderness to be tempted by the devil" (Matt 4:1). The Greek here has an infinitive of purpose: the Spirit of God leads Jesus into the wilderness *in order* that the devil may test him. We need to interpret the meaning of the sixth petition in light of this textual background.

It is clear that God does not do evil and does not tempt to the doing of wrong. The devil does that. But God can certainly bring those God has chosen into a situation in which they are confronted with the Evil One and all his seductive power. The temptation story in the gospels further shows that this testing, this confrontation with evil, is closely connected with God's calling. We should interpret the sixth petition of the Our Father on that basis also.

"Lead us not into temptation" can therefore not be intended superficially and directly, as if it meant to ask that God not test us at all, for God led both Abraham and Jesus into situations of testing, and it happens again and again in the Bible that God tests individuals or the whole people.

Consequently, the petition can only mean: "Lead us not into a situation of testing beyond our strength!

Lead us not into a situation in which the power of evil is stronger than we are!" This corresponds precisely to the Syriac Anaphora of St. James, in which, after the end of the Our Father, the priest continues: "Yea, Lord our God, enter us not into intolerable temptation, but deliver us from the evil one, making a way of escaping from temptation." The Anaphora of St. James draws its phrasing at this point from a Pauline text that again points us to the right explanation of the sixth petition of the Our Father. In 1 Corinthians 10:1-10, Paul speaks of the testing of Israel in the wilderness. He then continues:

> These things happened to them to serve as an example, and they were written down to instruct us, on whom the ends of the ages have come. So if you think you are standing, watch out that you do not fall. No testing has overtaken you that is not common to everyone [i.e., that is not beyond human resistance]. God is faithful, and . . . will not let you be tested beyond your strength, but with the testing . . . will also provide the way out so that you may be able to endure it. (1 Cor 10:11-13)

What is so remarkable about that text? It says that God certainly allows us to fall into temptation and even *creates* the test, that is, the situation within which we are tempted. But "with the testing," behind which the evil tempter may indeed lie (cp. 1 Thess 3:5; 1 Cor 7:5), God also creates the way out: God takes care that we are not tested beyond our capabilities, that we are not conquered by temptation, that we do not succumb to it. That is exactly what is asked in the sixth petition of the Our Father.

But let us return to the story of Jesus' temptation in the wilderness. We can learn even more from it about the right interpretation of the sixth petition. What is the issue here? It is whether Jesus will fall away or remain faithful to his mission. That is: it is not about something peripheral, just *any* test, but about holding fast to his own calling. So let us look more closely at Jesus' temptation as described by Matthew:

> Then Jesus was led up by the Spirit into the wilderness to be tempted by the devil. He fasted forty days and forty nights, and afterwards he was famished. The tempter came and said to him, "If you are the Son of God, command these stones to become loaves of bread." But he answered, "It is written,
>
> > 'One does not live by bread alone,
> > > but by every word that comes from the mouth of God.'"

Then the devil took him to the holy city and
placed him on the pinnacle of the temple, saying to him, "If you are the Son of God, throw
yourself down; for it is written,

> 'He will command his angels concerning
> you,'
> and 'On their hands they will bear you
> up,
> so that you will not dash your foot against
> a stone.' "

Jesus said to him, "Again it is written, 'Do not
put the Lord your God to the test.' "

Again, the devil took him to a very high
mountain and showed him all the kingdoms
of the world and their splendor; and he said
to him, "All these I will give you, if you will
fall down and worship me." Jesus said to him,
"Away with you, Satan! for it is written,

> 'Worship the Lord your God,
> and serve only him.' "

Then the devil left him, and suddenly angels
came and waited on him. (Matt 4:1-11)

This temptation story is a very carefully con-
sidered composition. Three times the tempter approaches Jesus. Three times he seeks to persuade him
to deviate from his call. Three times Jesus replies with
a saying from the Bible showing that he remains true

to that call. So this text is not simply about temptations, to which all human beings are exposed—greed, or arrogance, or grasping at power.

Instead, this is about the fundamental sin of the people of God, the specific temptation that confronts believers in particular. Those who have dared the exodus and set their feet on the path of faith are not tested less than others, but more. The temptation into which the people of God repeatedly enter extends much deeper than the ordinary immorality of society. The temptation of the people of God, and so also that of Jesus, is rooted in the *call itself*—at the center of what Israel was chosen to do: to live in the world as a people that gives honor to God alone, acknowledges God as its only Ruler, so that all may see and discern in this people what God intends for the world.

But when the people of God do not live for God but for themselves, when they do not seek God's honor but their own, and when in the process God even becomes an instrument for the accomplishment of their own interests, then the call and the mission are perverted at their very center. Then self-promotion replaces proclamation and self-serving takes the place of service to others.

It is no accident that Israel's time in the wilderness echoes especially in the temptation story—above all, certainly, in the number forty. Israel's sojourn in the wilderness is seen in the Old Testament not only as the time of its betrothal to God but also as a time of education and testing for the people. Deuteronomy 8:2-3 reads:

> Remember the long way that the LORD your God has led you these forty years in the wilderness, in order to humble you, testing you to know what was in your heart, whether or not you would keep his commandments. . . . [He wanted to] make you understand that one does not live by bread alone, but by every word that comes from the mouth of the LORD.

We are immediately struck by the features common to this text and the temptation story in Matthew 4:1-11. So let us look a little more closely at the story, which presents in the most sublime form the sin of those called:

> *First scene:* People use the opportunities offered by the mission to be God's people in order to serve their own interests instead. Image: People acquire bread for themselves.
> *Second scene:* People do not serve God but themselves by creating their own scenario and even misuse Sacred Scripture for their own purposes.

*Third scene:* Ultimately, people seek power and glory for themselves. They try to exercise control over others. They use their offices as a means to make themselves more prominent than others. There is scarcely any temptation greater than that of seeking to control others, especially through moral pressure that deprives them of freedom, and spiritual power that seeks not to serve but to be served. And then emerges most clearly what is happening at depth in the whole process: those who serve not God but themselves are serving the devil.

Only when we understand how narrow and dangerous is the way to giving God the glory, and how swiftly the very faith of those called sinks into self-preservation, self-staging, a making of oneself to be master—only then do we understand the explosive point of the temptation story: the very ones who are called and commissioned by God can use their calling in order to serve only themselves.

What is so terrifying and at the same time so consoling is that even Jesus was tempted by all that, to the very depths of his being. But he withstood the tempter. Our story shows that he does so not by his own strength but by holding fast to the word of God. That is why he thrice cites Sacred Scripture, which is Israel's collective knowledge of how to make the distinction, how to decide.

We too are tempted. Or do we really believe that Jesus was tempted and we will not be? For us too, the most dangerous temptations will always be against the calling we have received as Christians: against building community, against gathering the people of God. We will not be able to resist these temptations, which always bear a pale shimmer of plausibility, unless we too rely on the knowledge assembled by the people of God, preserved for us in Scripture and the church's tradition.

It cannot have been accidental that Jesus taught his disciples—those who had left their families and followed him—to pray in the Our Father "and lead us not into temptation!" He knew that the greatest danger for his disciples was that they might pervert their calling. No one escapes that temptation: it is even a necessary testing so that faith may be entirely pure. But the disciples may and must pray to God: "Lead us not into a situation that will be too hard for us! Lead us not into a situation in which temptation will overcome us!"

Quite unexpectedly, our interpretation of the sixth petition in the Our Father brought us to Israel's situation in the wilderness: as Jesus was tested by God in the desert, so God had already tested Israel in the desert. In that connection I quoted Deuteronomy 8:2: "Remember the long way that the LORD your God has led you these forty years in the wilderness, in order to humble you, testing you to know what was in your heart, whether or not you would keep his commandments."

But since we have already seen how the story of the manna relates to the fourth petition of the Our Father, and here the wilderness situation appears in relation to the sixth petition, the question arises: can it be that the second part of the Our Father looks back much more intensely than we thought to the Pentateuch, and especially to the books of Exodus and Deuteronomy? In that case the fifth petition, for forgiveness of sins, would also have to be located within the wilderness narrative. In fact, that is not only possible but obvious.

The breach of the covenant in Exodus 32 is altogether central to the complex of wilderness narratives in the book of Exodus. Israel had scarcely received the Torah at Sinai, God had just barely concluded the covenant with Israel, when the people immediately broke the covenant and danced before the golden calf. That is nothing other than the perversion of its calling, an apostasy from God.

After that apostasy of Israel, Moses became the speaker for the whole people. He reminds God of the oath God had sworn to their ancestors (Exod 32:11-14). At the climax of his advocacy for Israel, Moses prays to God: "Although this is a stiff-necked people, pardon our iniquity and our sin, and take us [again] for your inheritance" (Exod 34:9). And God forgives Israel's sin and makes a new beginning with them. In evaluating this event we have to say that this is not about *just any* sin; it is the primal temptation and primal sin of Israel: apostasy from its God. At that point we are immediately faced with the second part of the Our Father, because it too, as we saw, is not about just any trespass but about the great sin of apostasy from one's own calling.

As a result we observe a deeper internal connection: both the bread petition and the one for forgiveness of sins, as well as the theme of testing by God, have the stories of Israel in the wilderness as their background. As the people of God was once led by God in a wilderness situation, so it is now with Jesus' disciples. They have left everything. They are on an uncertain journey. They receive the bread they need for each day. God forgives their sin: the sin of betraying their proper calling. And the whole thing is a situation of testing in which the disciples' faith must prove itself genuine.

Thus Jesus shaped the prayer of his disciples entirely against a biblical background: the first three petitions based on the theology of three of the great prophets (Ezekiel, Daniel, and Isaiah), and the next three with the aid of the Pentateuch, especially against the background of the wilderness narratives in the book of Exodus.

With what intensity must Jesus have read Scripture! With what power did he himself follow the path of Israel, now in pure obedience to the will of the Father! And with what passion does he desire that his disciples also follow that path, the long road of Israel!

# 9. Liberation from Evil

IN LUKE'S VERSION the Our Father ends with the petition: "Lead us not into temptation." Matthew's version expands that petition with the clause "but deliver us from evil." This expansion is often counted in Christian tradition as a seventh petition although, to be precise, we should regard it as a final clause of the sixth. Early Christian interpreters loved the number seven.

The Greek text leaves open the question whether this petition refers to "evil" or "the evil one." What should we envision when we say the conclusion to the Our Father—the devil or the evil in the world, such as hatred between nations, the exploitation of the poor, the deep-seated structures of oppression?

It is always good to allow oneself to be guided by the church in such matters. How does the church understand the seventh petition of the Our Father? The New Testament itself gives us a first indication.

Besides the two versions of the Our Father in Matthew and Luke we can identify a number of texts that reflect the Lord's Prayer. Thus, for example, 2 Timothy clearly adopts the conclusion of the Our Father: "The Lord will rescue me from every evil attack and save me for his heavenly kingdom. To him be the glory forever and ever. Amen" (2 Tim 4:18).

The author of that letter, probably a member of Paul's circle of coworkers, not only knew the Our Father and its final petition but already ends it with a doxology. But what is important here is that he does not interpret rescue from evil directly in terms of the devil but primarily in regard to the evil realities of the world.

We find a second indication in the eucharistic celebration, which from a very early date contained an addition, the so-called embolism, between the seventh petition and the doxology. That addition at first clings to the seventh petition, meditating on and interpreting it. In *The Roman Missal* (2011) it reads:

> Deliver us, Lord, we pray, from every evil,
> graciously grant peace in our days,
> that, by the help of your mercy,
> we may be always free from sin
> and safe from all distress,
> as we await the blessed hope
> and the coming of our Savior, Jesus Christ.

This extraordinarily compact text interprets the seventh petition of the Our Father not in terms of the Evil One but in reference to *evil*: that from which we ask to be freed is the sum of the terrible realities of this world, namely, strife, discord, hatred, violence—the things that are diametrically opposed to peace. They are the results of "sin." God is asked to deliver us from these evil realities and give us peace—the peace that frees the world "forever" from the power of sin and from the distress and confusion that come into the world through sin.

It is clear that this is not about a little more peace or a little less sin but about the complete *eschatological* peace in which all sin and all distress will be overcome.

But how does that eschatological peace enter the world? It does so with the return of Jesus Christ. The text of the embolism here alludes to the letter to Titus, which in 2:13 speaks of the end-time return of "our savior, Jesus Christ," as our "blessed hope." Thus the seventh petition of the Our Father holds fast to the situation, because the Lord's Prayer is formulated, from beginning to end, against an *eschatological* horizon. The gathering of the people of God, the coming of God's reign, and the fulfillment of God's plan for history are eschatological events. Certainly the

embolism understands the Our Father not only escha-
tologically but christologically as well. Jesus Christ
is the one in whom everything beseeched in the Our
Father is fulfilled.

And when is it fulfilled? Not only in his return at
the end of time but already "in our days," as the embolism explicitly says. Christ's return does not happen only at the end of the world but, in anticipation,
in the present, whenever the Eucharist is celebrated.
His return takes place when, following the embolism,
we pray for peace in the church and then share that
peace with all those participating in the celebration.
When those present accept that proclamation, extend it to one another, and then receive the Eucharist together, the eschatological peace begins now in
the church, and it is to extend beyond the church to
encompass the whole world.

Thus the expansion of the Our Father in the embolism has grasped the meaning of the Lord's Prayer with
the greatest accuracy. We may rely on this ecclesial-
liturgical interpretation when we pray the Our Father.

# 10. Desperate Cry and Confident Trust

WHETHER THE LAST CLAUSE of the Our Father as Jesus spoke it was "lead us not into temptation" or "deliver us from evil," it ends abruptly. It breaks off with a desperate cry. Such a prayer ending was so foreign to the mentality of Jewish prayer at that time that a doxology was very quickly added to round off the ending of the Our Father: "For the kingdom, the power, and the glory are yours, now and forever. Amen."

The seventh petition in Matthew's version may also have been an early attempt to soften the abrupt ending we find in Luke—an ending that is not only unusual but chilling. But Jesus may have intended just such a conclusion to the prayer: in it he would have expressed in the *form* of the prayer the distress of the one praying—that is, of a disciple of Jesus—but also that of the people of God and of God's cause.

Apparently we are unable, by ourselves, to see the true misery of the world, and especially not the extreme distress of the people of God, which is supposed to be the place where paradise is already shining forth, the place where God's reign is already flowering in the world. Instead, we continually obliterate this will of God for salvation. We do so by hallowing our own names and not the name of God; by not acknowledging God's rule but wanting to be our own masters; by not entering into God's plan but serving our private interests; by not trusting, without security, that on the coming day God will care for us, relying instead on our own provision for our lives.

We hinder the coming of the reign of God by refusing to forgive, insisting rigidly and proudly on our own rights. Above all, we do so by constantly being unfaithful to our calling. That is the misery of the people of God. That is why the Our Father is pure petition and why it ends with a cry.

In light of this critical situation, the Our Father's intention is to gather disciples and strengthen them in their existence as such. The Our Father's desire is that the gathering and sanctification of the people of God may become our foremost concern. It desires that we not be troubled about the success of our own plans but concern ourselves with the success of God's plan. It wants God to be master, not we ourselves. It desires that every member of the people of God help the others: those who follow Jesus directly and those who assist them. It wants us to forgive each other our sins every day. It desires, ultimately, to make us aware how immediately each of us is in danger of falling away from faith.

Those who have grasped what the Our Father really says must know that it has consequences. It is a dangerous prayer, and still we can pray it—because this prayer also contains enormous confidence, which begins with the very first word, *Abba*, the familiar address to the father stemming from the intimate circle of the family. That confidence also comes, however, from the knowledge that God's plan will succeed because God's word does not return to God empty. And it is connected with the insight that God's mercy is without limit. When people wholeheartedly forgive one another's sins, can there be any doubt that God forgives? That is why the Our Father is a prayer filled with trust. Every baptized person may pray it, also and especially those who have understood their guilt and recognized how far they are from true discipleship of Jesus. And that means all of us.

# 11. A Paraphrase of the Our Father

*N*OW THAT WE HAVE REACHED the end of the book, let us go back to the beginning! We saw at least a sampling of the countless paraphrases of the Our Father—short ones and long ones, some true to the text and some that run beyond it, those that follow the meaning and those that change it, those that are reverent and those that are provocative. I am almost afraid to add still another paraphrase of the Our Father to all the rest.

Perhaps, though, it is appropriate to do so, because it makes sense to summarize the most important lines of interpretation described in this book. It makes sense to do so as briefly as possible. And it makes sense that the genre, namely, that of "petition," not be abandoned. Of course, I also need to say as clearly as possible what the following paraphrase is *not*.

It is in no way a prayer that anyone should pray. That is not its purpose. It is simply intended to interpret the Our Father in the briefest possible form. It is an aid to understanding. Even those who pray the Our Father privately should pray it in its official form as given by the church.

My paraphrase also does not replace what has been said in the previous ten chapters. It became clear there that Jesus shaped the prayer for his disciples against the background of the theology of the great prophets, and even central texts of the Torah, especially the book of Exodus. A brief paraphrase can in no way place that whole background before our eyes. Only when we are clear about all that can we, perhaps, formulate our paraphrase as follows:

Father in heaven, we are your disciples, your community, your church. Together with Jesus, and listening to his words, we are permitted to speak to you as our father. *Abba*, dear Father!

Gather your scattered and strife-torn people. Make it to be the true people of God, so that your name may be honored before all the world. Give us the strength to gather a community in your name, to bring it together and make it one. Hallowed be your name!

Let your reign, your rule come into the world. Be our only Master. We no longer want to serve our self-made gods. Give us the strength to live as truly human, as your people, without violence or hatred, in your peace. Your kingdom come!

Bring your plan to completion, the plan for the world you have conceived from all eternity. Let it come from heaven to earth, from your heart to ours. Give us the strength, together with our communities, to be your aid, your sacrament for the world. Your will be done!

Because you are our dear Father, give us today as much of the essentials as necessary for the day to come. Let our first concern be for your reign, and let it be more important to us than everything else. Let us be so filled with the need to bear witness to it that we have no time at all to plan and constantly to think only of ourselves. Give us the strength, in all this, to help one another and provide for one another. Give us today the bread we need!

We can never repay all the debts we have incurred before you, and to which we continually add. We always fall short in love. Therefore: forgive us all our indebtedness, all our guilt!

We know that we dare not utter such a prayer unless we also forgive our brothers and sisters all their debts to us. Forgive us our debts as we forgive our debtors!

It is because your reign is to break into our miserable history that we are so threatened by temptation: the temptation to fall away, to surrender our discipleship, to doubt your church and no longer believe in your plan for the world. Do not lead us into a situation in which this great temptation will overcome us. Let us not fall victim to it, but deliver us from the deadly power of evil!

Let me say again that such a paraphrase cannot replace the Our Father. Jesus' prayer is better. It does not use many words. It is brief and incisive. Its vividness comes from the very fact that there is no need to say many words to God. God knows what we need before we ask (Matt 6:7-8).

We should pray the Our Father every day, as Jesus taught it and the church has handed it down to us—pray it slowly, thoughtfully, and reverently. We should protect it like a costly treasure. It not only leads us to the center of our Christian existence; it also shows us who Jesus really was, because it draws us to the center of his heart.

# REFERENCES AND ACKNOWLEDGMENTS

*Chapter 1*

"The Amidah Prayer: A New Translation," by David Bivin, at http://www.egrc.net/articles/other/amidah.html.

Akkadian prayer of "raising the hands" at https://www.bibliotecapleyades.net/sitchin/sitchinbooks01_02.htm.

For the Kaddish see, *inter alia*, ReformJudaism.org, https://reformjudaism.org/practice/prayers-blessings/mourners-kaddish.

*Chapter 4*

Cosy Piéro, "Anschlag des mündigen Gebets an das Portal der Theatinerkirche München" (1992); see http://www.cosypiero.de/vita.html. Translation Linda M. Maloney.

"The Eighteen Benedictions" (*Shemoneh Esreh*), at https://www.tzion.org/articles/EighteenBenedictions.htm.

A benediction "against slanderers," supposedly added at the Council of Jamnia (ca. 70–90 CE?), makes the petitions number nineteen.

## Chapter 6

John Chrysostom, *Homilies on Matthew*, from *Nicene and Post-Nicene Fathers*, 1st ser., vol. 10 (Buffalo, NY: Christian Literature Publishing Co., 1888.) Revised and edited for New Advent by Kevin Knight. Available at http://www.newadvent.org/fathers/200119.htm.

Matthias Claudius, quoted in a review of his *Sämtliche Werke* in *The New York Review* 5, 9 (New York, 1839), 195–96.

For a fuller explication of the interpretation of the third petition see Gerhard Lohfink, "Der präexistente Heilsplan. Sinn und Hintergrund der dritten Vaterunserbitte," in *Studien zum Neuen Testament*, SBAB.NT 5 (Stuttgart: Katholisches Bibelwerk, 1989), 49–75.

## Chapter 8

"Anaphora of St. James," available at http://sor.cua.edu/Liturgy/Anaphora/James.html.

My brother Norbert's essays on the Our Father are collected in Georg Braulik and Norbert Lohfink, *Liturgie und Bibel. Gesammelte Aufsätze* (Frankfurt am Main: Peter Lang, 2005). In particular, I owe a very great deal to his essay, "Das Vaterunser, intertextuell gebetet," pp. 343–65 in that volume, in which he develops the Old Testament background of the Our Father in the Prophets and the Pentateuch.